Always By Your Side

GAYNOR CARRILLO

3

ISBN: 1493560573

ISBN-13: 978-1493560578

DEDICATION

To my wonderful children Nicole and Danny,
I love you both endlessly. I always will do, in this
world and beyond.

To my husband, for always being by my side.

To my mother, who I love unconditionally.

I will always be by your side.

ACKNOWLEDGMENTS

It would be impossible to thank all those living and passed who have helped me in my life. If you know me in any way, then you have touched my life and you are one of the many people I thank from the bottom of my heart.

I must thank my dear darling Nana Wasdell, for loving me in such a way that even now, I still feel the love. Her love for me, I will pass down throughout many generations

My uncle Donald, who throughout my childhood has always cared for me and protected me.

My aunty Janet for showing me fun and kindness for many of my younger years. What a truly wonderful woman and inspiration you are.

I also have to thank my dear departed friend Dee for being my guide in many ways; I am unsure where I would be without your constant guidance.

My cousin Amanda, whom I love and cherish like a sister. I thank you Amanda for always being there and never judging me, just loving me the way I am.

Very special thanks to my friend Beli. You are my inspiration and my reflection. Thank you for the endless hours you listened to me and helped me find my answers.

I need to give a huge thanks to my aunty Linda Wasdell for helping me with the maze of letters and dots. Sacrificing her holiday to help me reach my dream.

Linda Clark: Thank you wherever you are, those first classes were important for me.

Joanne Jopling: As strong as a nettle yet as gentle as a sailing Angel, I thank you for all the times you just listened.

Kerry Mckeown: Thank you, you will always be in my heart. The circle of friendship that never ends. What magic we found!

Leah Carpenter: I can still see us, walking up the hill with ten bottles of wine, only nine made it home, just as sisters do. Thank you.

Yeshim and Tolga Tugsat: I can't wait to see you both again. You will both always be a part of me.

Nicola O'Rourke: How time has flown. Thank you for being my childhood friend. Time will never change our friendship.

This book would be nothing more than empty pages if it was not for the wonderful Spirits I have had the privilege of meeting throughout my lifetime. I thank and treasure each encounter.

My shining light, Micheal. I thank you forever and thereafter.
Ozzar, for always standing in the background.

Dave, Granddad, Brian, Wendy, Ronnie, Ron, Mehmet, Dee, Pamela, Andres, Rick. "Till we meet again."

Daniel. Judy. Carmen. Antony. Marc. Jack. Floyd. Miguel. Joseph
Dave. Heidy's dad. Francisco. Alejandro. Pepe. Maria. Thomas.
Tanya. Teresa. Julia. Marie. Manoli. Monica. Ricardo. Daisy.
Pamela. Xavier. Ana. Dolly. Beatrice. Mikel. Kelvin. Patrick.
Antonio. Adolfo. Rick. Juan.
Rosario. Racheal. Pilli. Marie Carmen. Maria Del mar. Petre.
Rosier. Rosa. Sonia. Olga. Maria del pueblo. Chari. Marie Angeles.
Asuncion. Diane. Velma. Isabel. Rocio. Neuss. Sammy. Lolly.
Merce. Joan. Delores. Marebelle. Ana Marie. Gorki. Antonia. Eva.
Suzanna. Flora. Laura. Nate. Anna. Jordi (William). Fina.
Sandra. Macarena. Estella. Gemma. Montserrat. Rita. Juan.

Yolanda. Tamara. Maria Delores. Christina. Raffa. Natalia. Kim.

Melba. Paki. Zarah. Maria Rosa. Conception. Esperanza. Pure.
Julia. Marta. Francesca. Larry. William. Rosa. Ann. Angeles.
Fatima. Pillar. Jessica. Jose. Ines. Dorrie. Ellen. Luisa. Santi.
Debbie. Juana. Estrella. Jesus. Josefa. Nicola. Bridget. Victoria.
Ian. Consuelo. Paquita. Mercedes. Jason. Sofia. Incarnation.
Chelo. Beatriz. Conchi. Paz. Trinidad. Ivy. Vera. Nora. Mr Davis.
Coral. Elaine. Maisy. Beatty. Heidi. Sarah. Charlie. Lauren.
Paula. Jane. Juan Carlos. Rosario. Richard. Silvia. Alexandra.
Micheal. Conchi. Gracia. Lisa. Arturo. Trinity. Fernanda.
Susie. Manuela. Bethem. Mirta. Emma. Sabastian. Fina. Wiz.
Magda. Juanita. Karen. Imma. Montsy. Jodie. Edwardo. Belen.
Ester. Marina. Matitlda. Kathy. Liz. Susan. Sam. Joanne. Claire.
Sherly. Evan. Ethel. Jimmy. Makala. Mary. Mandy. Teresa. Jean.
John. Niko. Lorrain. Pat. The entire Garcia family. The list is
endless…

**A special thank you to all who have given permission for me
to include you in my book. Thank you all.**

CONTENTS

Part one

"The Place"

Part two

In Between Worlds

Part Three

Their stories

Part One

"The Place"

Chapter 1

My Childhood in Wonderland

I was an unplanned pregnancy, born in the north of England into a lower class family. My Nana, my mum's mum, had nine children and I had an endless amount of cousins, aunts, and uncles. It was a large family and although I was an only child, family constantly surrounded me.

I have a clear childhood memory, one that I never really thought much about until I realized not many people remember such details about their childhood as I do. I remember being a small baby in my cot and waking up crying because of dreams I had, very vivid dreams.

I have always dreamed at night, but one recurring dream stood out more than the rest, a dream where I would see myself in an entirely different place. I just called it "The Place," because for years I did not quite understand where I was. It was a kind of wonderland.

This wonderland was similar to the world I was living in, yet at the same time so very different. It was a magical place, where flowers would dance and trees would talk to me, the grass would grow around my feet, it was a familiar place full of peace and beauty. In addition, the people I met there were always full of love and laughter, I would dream often of "The Place," yet I knew it was not in my world. I knew my way around "The Place," very well. I also made friends there and each time I returned in my dreams I would see my friends or meet new ones. I always awoke with a feeling of peace.

I also suffered and still do, with out of body experiences. Often when I sleep, I will suddenly find myself outside my body, floating in the air. Whilst travelling without my body, I can see and hear everything below me as I float through the air. Unfortunately, I never really go anywhere exciting, normally I only go as far as the next room.

These episodes didn't only happen whilst sleeping. I remember once I was lying on the sofa, I was tired and cold and I didn't want to move, yet I knew I had to get up. Suddenly I found myself floating in the air. I floated through the wall and outside, as I floated I saw people below me. In the midst of the people, I saw one of my cousin's. I flew closer to him and I noticed everything he was wearing and noticed he was heading in the direction of where I was staying at the time. I then floated briefly around the park and then back to the sofa. I wondered how I was supposed to return into my body. My body looked like I was sleeping as I was just lying there on the sofa, as soon as I thought about it I was back inside my body again. It felt very real.

Shortly after I returned to my body, there was a knock on the door, it was my cousin, and he was wearing the exact same clothes I had just seen him in as I had floated above him. These flying episodes would happen randomly.

My parents had separated shortly after my first birthday. The relationship was not working out between them. My mum became a single working mum therefor I started sleeping more and more at my Nana's house as my mum's working hours were early and long.

My Nana's house was a large three bedroomed house in Manchester on one of the biggest council estates in Europe. It was also full of family and of Spirit. I do not ever remember a time in my life when I started to see Spirit. I just know there was never a time I remember not seeing them. I never really made much of a fuss about it. Seeing Spirits was normal to me as a child, so was dreaming things that would later happen along with talking to people in my head. People would talk to me and I would often hear them in my mind and I would answer them, I had long and short conversations for as long as I can remember all happening inside my own mind. It was a long time before I realized the people I was hearing in my mind, were Spirit people. It seemed I was living in a multiplicity of worlds, the physical and the Spirit world.

I would see random Spirits appear and disappear. This would happen anywhere. I may have walked into my bedroom at my Nana's house to do something and as I walked in I would see a random Spirit person just standing there, and before my eyes, they would often disappear. The question of why I was seeing Spirit at no point crossed my childhood mind.

My aunty Janet was the youngest of my Nana's children, she was still living at home, in my Nana's house. I loved being with her. She had long red hair and perfect white teeth. My aunty was the most beautiful woman I had ever seen and she would play with me for hours, take me to parks, talk to me, and play music and dance. She was a very creative person and she loved sharing her time with me. I remember the classical music she would play and her dancing around like a ballerina.

My aunty Janet took me to my first playschool. I played as all the other girls did. Anyone who would have seen me playing on the big green mat would have thought I was just any ordinary little girl. I tried to fit in, although I always seemed to feel like the odd one out. I felt somewhat detached from this world. I was unsure why I was here. Although I never questioned the reason behind the feeling, it was just something I felt. I wondered why my aunty Janet would leave me at the school and return to pick me up later, why didn't she just stay. I was told because only the teacher could stay. I remember clearly being confused because I saw so many adults in class.

I didn't understand why all the children had family members stay with them throughout the class, some had their Nanas and

Granddads, some had uncles and aunts, yet Janet would leave me alone. I would often cry and beg her not to leave me, it wasn't because I didn't like it there, it was because it frustrated me that everyone seemed to be lying to me. "Adults are not allowed to stay," Janet would tell me repeatedly, often with the backup of the teacher who would agree with her, yet I would look around and see a whole classroom full of children and adults.

I was very confused and because I was so young I didn't know how to say what I was feeling, instead of asking why I could see so many adults in the class instead I would cry. I spent the remaining days of playschool refusing to return.

My mum would often take me to visit her eldest sister, my aunty Diane in Wales. I loved going there. Diane lived with her husband Dave, and I was very close to my cousins Dawn and Dayne. Dave was a fireman and he would often come home from work with bags of sweets and chocolates for me and my cousins. He knew I liked Cadburys cream eggs and would always make sure there was one in the bag for me. The family all lived in a bungalow in North Wales and it was a home that I remember full of fun and laughter. Dave would come home from work, tickle us all, and throw us over his shoulder whilst we all screamed with laughter.

Dayne and I had a special relationship and I often suspected he could also see things others couldn't see. One day at my Nana's house, he came running down the stairs claiming he had seen an old lady sat in a rocking chair in my Nana's bedroom. He described the lady, warts and all. It seemed everyone recognized her yet Dayne had never met her. I ran into the bedroom after Dayne, yet I saw no one, no old lady in a rocking chair. I wondered what kind of magic powers Dayne possessed to see people I could not see. He would also casually say things to me that made me feel that he also was living in his own wonderland.

Dawn had an imaginary friend for a long time before I was born, it became an issue as she would talk to her friend often. Her friend was called Gaynor and had left Dawn's life just before I was born.

Growing up I asked Dawn a few times if she remembered her imaginary friend and she would often tell me how she remembered a figure always dressed in black.

Maybe it was these strange occurrences that brought me closer to Dawn and Dayne or maybe it was the stability and love that was in their home.

I noticed my mum was crying a lot and she and my other aunts would often shut up when I walked into a room.

Finally, my mum sat me down and explained to me that my uncle Dave had gone to Heaven to live with the Angels, she pointed to the sky as if to show me he was way up there in the clouds.

I was very young at the time, but I remember thinking, is this the best she could come up with?

I asked her what had happened and she told me he had got cancer, I knew cancer was a bad word as every time an adult said it they would whisper it, but I had no concept of illness. I remember crying because everyone else around me was crying, but it wasn't until my mum took me to visit my aunty again when I realized what had happened.

On entering the bungalow, I knew everything had changed. There was an empty feeling, almost a coldness, and the look of grief on my cousin's faces told me that they were in so much pain, so young yet their eyes told me their world had changed forever. It was my first brush with grief.

My Nana had a friend who lived on the same street as her, a very old lady with pure white hair. She lived in a huge house, yet due to illness had become confined only to the downstairs. Her bed lay centre stage in her living room. She was a tealeaf reader and my Nana would go visit her and have a cup of tea. The lady would then read my Nana's tea leaves. I loved going to visit her with my Nana. This frail old lady, to me as a child, had magic powers. She was able to see things in the teacup I could not, pictures, and signs with meanings often seen in my Nana's cups of tea became translated into important information about my Nana's future. I was so intrigued with her knowledge that I started to drink tea whilst I visited there with the hope she would one day also read my tealeaves. She never did, yet I will never forget how much of an impact she had on me. To me she was magical. I wanted magic powers like her, I wanted to be able to see things about people's future.

My Nana owned a big green book full of spells and rituals and all things occult. I would hear my Nana and my aunties reading pages from the book on occasion. The green book was often pulled out and my Nana would read something in it, tell one of my aunts and I would see a smile in their eyes, as if they knew something they shouldn't. The book was mainly about predicting the future through signs, omens and creating spells.

I began to beg Janet and my Nana to read me the book. I also wanted to know things about people's future, I wanted to learn how to see signs and omens. For some unknown reason, they did pass some time reading that big green book to me. I was so young I should not have understood a single word of it, yet surprisingly I did. Soon they became bored reading the same book and they would take out the big children's storybook from my Nana's old cabinet and read that to me instead, so I decided to learn to read. Amazingly, I did. At a very young age, I was reading very well. Well enough to get on a chair, pull out the green book and read parts of it to myself. I was mostly intrigued with the Tarot chapters of the book. There was also a part about reading the future with poker cards. I did not have Tarot cards, but in my Nana's bottom drawer, there were many packs of poker cards. That was my next new hobby. I spent hours as a little girl trying to read the future with poker cards. My dream was to become a Tarot reader.

I have always had a voice talk to me, mainly a voice inside my own mind, but often I would see the man it belonged to, a slim man with a long hair. He had the most calming and piercing eyes. He had always been around me since I could remember. Even when I couldn't see him I knew he was there. I never questioned who he was. To me, he was just a man who was always around me, a friend. I also knew he was different, there was something special about him that I couldn't quite work out. At any chosen time, I could talk to him and hear him, often in my own mind. I would mostly talk to him about silly things. I often called him my friend or the voice in my head. I now call this voice in my head Micheal.

My cousin Amanda often slept over at my Nana's house. We were very close, almost like sisters, and one night whilst we were in bed, she started shaking with fear and said she could see a ghost. I looked around the dark room and the only person I could see was a Spirit man standing by the window. I couldn't see a ghost. Amanda had pointed to where the Spirit man was and said, "There," I looked again, yet still I could only see the Spirit man standing by the window. "Do you mean the man stood by the window?" I asked. "Yes," she cried and placed her head under the blankets. "This house is haunted," she whispered to me from under the blankets.

I laid in my bed wondering what was happening. Why was she scared of the man and why had she called him a ghost? Surely she had seen him many times, he was always around my Nana's house? I was puzzled by her fear.

I asked Micheal why Amanda had been so scared, he explained to me that some people were scared of the unknown.

Looking back on my childhood, I find it hard to believe that nobody in my huge family noticed anything different about me. If I hid my double life, it was not intentional.

I hated school and I found it completely boring. The only thing that interested me was when I sat in front of the teachers. Somehow, I found a way of being able to switch my mind off from the lesson so I was not listening to a word the teachers were saying and at the same time, I would relax and see the many colours that surrounded the teachers. Later I found out these colours were called auras. At the time, I just knew them as the colours around people. I could see the colours around anyone but I only did it with my teachers because I had to sit in front of them in class, it was my way of passing the time.

I would see spectrums of colours and I understood at the time why each teacher's colours would often change. Moreover, some teacher's auras would often expel the same colour all the time. As I was always moving schools I could never remember the names of teachers so I would give them their aura names, Mr Orange, Mrs Yellow, Mrs Green and so forth.

I also learnt how to meditate during class, I would sit quietly, and my eyes would look at the teacher, yet inside my mind, I would be in a completely different place. I started to transport myself, often going to "The Place," I went to in my dreams. I didn't know at the time I was meditating, I just knew I was no longer sat in a classroom listening to math. Instead, I would be in a field, walking amongst yellow flowers or I would be walking along the beach. I would meet up with friends I met in my dreams, friends from "The Place," and we would walk around together or just sit together. Although my body was sitting in class, my mind was thrown into a different world.

Up until this point, I had only ever been to the magical "Place" in my dreams and now I found I could get there by meditating. I found it quite exciting.

I spent most of my days entering this other world with my eyes open, relaxing and enjoying each moment of it. Only to then have to come back to reality and back to the classroom.

One teacher told me once I seem to daydream a lot. I remember almost laughing and thinking to myself, daydream? If only you knew, I just spent the last hour sitting on a bench by a river watching the water flow by me instead of listening to your class about science.

In between dreaming each night, dreams that would often come true or dreaming I was in another place, country or even another place in time. I was meditating most days to try to pass the time at school, I was watching auras around my teachers out of boredom, and I was flying around and floating through walls at random moments. I was also seeing Spirits on a regular basis and talking to people in my head. Yet I still never questioned anything that was happening to me, or why I was doing these things.

My Granddad used to take me on long walks on most non-school days, we used to walk to Heaton Park in Manchester, and walk for miles all around the huge park and then back home again, and the walks would take hours. I loved being in nature, I would sit and make daisy chains, roll down the grassy hills, follow the butterflies in the fields. My Granddad would talk about plants and their healing abilities for hours. I was so young when we started these walks that I remember he used to push me in my pram at first, an orange plastic pram, then as I grew I would go in the pram and walk back, then I grew old enough to no longer need my pram. Although the walks were long and often tiring, I used to love them.

England is beautiful with all its nature and greenery and as a child, these walks influenced me a lot. I was very connected to nature and I somehow felt a part of nature.

Halfway home we would always stop at an old English pub. Granddad would have a beer and I would have a coke. We were never allowed to tell my Nana about our adventures as we were a low-income family and she would not have been happy if she found out we stopped at the pub for a drink. I was never allowed to tell her about the times we went on the tour bus around the park, we would buy a pie or a sandwich and ride at the top of the bus eating lunch, or the times we went to Heaton Park museum.

My Granddad would treat me to ice creams and packets of crisps, boat rides and pony rides. We would go and see the animals and buy food to feed them. Again, we were never to mention it to Nana. Heaton Park was in a way similar to "The Place," yet at the same time, it felt worlds away, as if the beauty of the park was diminished compared to the wonderland I would visit in my dreams.

My Nana was always in the kitchen cooking. In the back garden, my Granddad had created his own fruit and veg shop. We had everything growing, tomatoes, strawberries, cabbages, cauliflower, and all types of fruit and vegetables. Nana must have saved a fortune as she was always cooking food from the garden.

I used to watch her bake cakes and I would sit in the kitchen with her whilst she did all the cooking. My Nana loved me a lot. I was spoilt by her, she was kind and caring to me, she would hug me and cuddle me, she was always feeding me and she taught me how to spell my name, how to count and other basic things that I should have really learnt at school if I would have listened. I would stand on a chair and help her bake, and after dinner, we would sit and eat all the day's treats that we had baked together. She would share all the family gossip with me and we would watch her programmes together whilst I lay on the sofa with the fire burning and a blanket over me.

My Granddad also spoilt me, he was not a liked person in the family, a feared man, and I am sure my family all have their own horror stories about him. Nevertheless, he spoilt me. He taught me how to ride my bike, he was very happy the day he took my stabilizers off, and I could ride it with just two wheels. I did notice he would hardly talk to any of my other cousins and he never seemed to take them anywhere.

It was my mother who completely spoilt me as a child, she would work hard and spend all her money on me, buying me any toy I wanted. I always wore good clothes and expensive shoes, she would take me out for meals in expensive restaurants, she took me to London, and we went to see theatre shows like 42nd street and Gigi. I used to dance all the way home. My mum always tried to overcompensate for leaving me at my Nana's for long periods whilst she worked, so she would buy me anything I wanted and take me out to the best places, she would play with me for hours. I was always back and forth, living at my Nana's then living at my mum's. My mum was always in different places, she never stayed in the same home for more than a few months. So I moved around quite a lot.

I loved being with my mum. She would make me laugh all the time and we had some great times. Living with Nana was all about baking and saving money. One chicken would serve nine of us and the bones were then made into soup. Living with my mum was all about going out to restaurants, shopping until late. My mum was fun and full of life. The contrast was tremendous. Living with my Nana and living with my mum was like night and day.

My childhood intuition was very good, I just seemed to know things, often silly things like my mum would be working late and I was going to stay at my Nana's that night, or one of my cousins were going to turn up for a short visit or my Nana would make lemon curd tarts. Silly things that although they were insignificant I just knew were going to happen.

Once I was with a friend and her mum, we walked to the post office, it was along a country lane and there was no one else around. It was daytime so I waited outside whilst my friend went inside the post office with her mum. A small white van pulled up next to me and the man in the van asked me if I liked dogs, I told him I did, and I walked closer the van. He told me his dog had just had puppies and that if I did not take one he was going to have to kill the poor pup. I almost cried, he told me all about this tiny fluffy dog, and then he offered to give me the puppy so I could save its life. "Get in the van," he said as he opened the door.

As I was about to get into the van to go and pick up my new pup, he offered me a sweet. In that instant I heard my mum very loudly, shout at me. "Never get into a car with a stranger and never take sweets from a stranger." It was my mum's voice I was hearing yet I looked around me and saw nobody was there. I had heard my mum's voice so clearly, I could even sense her by my side, almost feeling her breath on my neck as she spoke to me. I stepped away from the van and told the man I was not getting into his car. I then quickly moved myself to the door of the post office and ran inside. The man appeared very angry with me and drove off.

I never told anyone about that incident at the time, to me, it was just another strange experience. Now I look back and wonder what would have happened to me that day if I had not heard my mum's voice. I was so convinced I wanted that puppy I was about to get into this stranger's van.

Chapter 2

Daisy Chains

Shortly after the incident with the man in the van, I was playing in my garden with my friend Daisy. We had been playing for a while when another friend of mine named Sharon came running into my back garden and we all began to play together, or so I had thought. After a while I became agitated with Sharon, I noticed she was ignoring Daisy and had not said a word to her. "Why are you not talking to Daisy?" I asked.

"Who's Daisy?" Sharon responded, tilting her head to the side and squinting her eyes at me.

"Daisy, my friend," I said pointing over to Daisy, who was sitting on the grass where we had been playing.

Sharon squashed her face up at me, looked extremely confused, and said, "Who are you talking about?"

"She can't see me," I heard Daisy whisper; she was now standing behind me.

"What do you mean she can't see you?" I demanded to know.

Daisy giggled a childish giggle and before she could say anymore, she disappeared before my eyes. I stood with my jaw open, staring at the empty space where my friend had been standing.

"What are you talking about?" Sharon now wanted to know, she was becoming annoyed with me and wanting to know who I was talking about.

"Oh nothing," I replied, shrugging off what had just happened. "I don't feel well, I'm going to go to bed," I said. Sharon left and I went to my room and lay on my bed.

I was not bothered that Daisy was a Spirit girl, I did not quite understand how it all worked anyhow. However, I was bothered that I had not known until today. I wondered how many other friends of mine were Spirit children. I didn't see Daisy again for a long time after that day and I began to worry if by talking about her, I had somehow gotten her into trouble, and I never saw her in my garden again. I wondered what was wrong with Sharon, why couldn't she see Daisy. I never saw myself as having a gift of seeing Spirit; instead, I wondered what was "wrong" with those who couldn't see Spirit.

Around a year later I was in "The Place," I was not asleep, I was just lying on my bed and I found myself suddenly transported to "The Place." I could hear children playing and I walked over near some trees and saw a group of children all around my age, they were playing with a kitten, at first, I noticed a friend of mine who lived a few doors down from my Nana. She smiled at me and I said hi, I turned and saw Daisy. She smiled at me, her eyes were deep blue, and her cheeks were rosy pink. I was happy to see her again, I sat, and played with them all for a while, we had a lot of fun. Then I heard my mum calling me. I left "The Place," got up off my bed and went downstairs to my mum who had dinner waiting for me.

The next day I was sleeping at my Nana's when the news reached us that my little friend who lived a few doors away from my Nana had died a few days earlier. I remember I had seen her in "The Place." We had been playing together, she was happy. I did not feel any loss about her death. As the funeral car drove past my Nana's house, everyone on the street stood outside their front doors to give their respects to the mother. The mother came out of her house and she was hysterical, she was so grief-stricken she could barely walk to the funeral car where the tiny coffin of her daughter had been placed. I stood outside watching her. I desperately wanted to run up to her and tell her not to cry, her daughter was ok. I had seen her and played with her, I knew she was happy. Instead, I just stood watching, feeling helpless, I would have many years to come where I would be able to pass on messages from Spirit, but this wasn't one of them.

Looking back, I am amazed at my own childhood experiences, randomly, nothing seems like a big deal, yet when I put them all together and lived them on a daily basis it was quite amazing what was happening to me. I was always very sure of what was happening to me, I was just equally unsure and often confused as to why it didn't seem to be happening to everyone else, why could I see things other people couldn't, why was I entering an entire other world and yet my physical body didn't move? I knew without a doubt that I could enter "The Place." I knew I could see people no one else could, what was happening to me was so real, yet why it was only happening to me was what intrigued me. I was more confused at others not being able to see Micheal then I was with the fact that I could see him. It bothered me more that I was alone in what I was seeing and hearing. The actual hearing or seeing things did not bother me, as it was all so natural.

I remember a time I was living in London. My mum had met a man from Cyprus, and she must have liked him a lot, as she married him. I lived in a house in Greenwich with his relatives, a lovely family with children who were all around my age. My mum had gone over to Cyprus with her new husband and I were to follow some months later. I was quite excited about going to Cyprus. I knew her husband was a rich man, who owned horses and land in Cyprus, yet my mum was taking a long time to send for me and I was becoming increasingly unhappy about it. I knew inside that something was wrong. I just knew something was not as we had expected. Finally, my mum realized I was no longer happy waiting. I couldn't go back to my Nana's as my Nana already thought I was in Cyprus. She would not have been happy knowing I had been living with a family in London, no matter how nice they were to me. Finally, the ticket arrived.

I was eight years old when I boarded the flight on my own from the UK to Cyprus. I was excited, yet my intuition told me my mum didn't really want me to fly out. The flight seemed to take for ages and finally the plane had a smooth landing.

I ran off the plane and excitedly looked around for my mum. It took me a while to realize she was not there. I could not find my mum anywhere in the airport. I knew there was something wrong. I also knew there was no way that my mum would not be at the other end to pick me up. I had often travelled alone from Manchester to London. My Nana would put me on the coach in Manchester, and my mum would take me off the coach at London. I knew how paranoid my mum was about me not leaving the coach until I could see her, so I knew she would never leave me on my own in an airport in Cyprus.

Finally, I approached a friendly looking woman in reception, and she looked at my ticket. I was not in Cyprus. I was in Turkey. There was a change over flight in Turkey to Cyprus that I did not know about. The woman in reception showed me where I had to go and indicated that I had little time left.

I ran around Istanbul airport looking for my flight, I was filled with panic. I was about to miss my flight and be stranded alone in Istanbul airport. The image forming in my mind of my mum waiting for me and me not being there made me feel sick. In all the haste, for some reason, I just stopped, right there in the airport with people pushing past me and everyone speaking loudly in a foreign language I just stopped. I stood still for a moment, I took a deep breath, and just for a moment, I became silent. Suddenly the noise of the airport disappeared, I did not notice the people pushing past me, nor any of the activity around me, and I just became silent. After a few moments, I open my eyes, and so very calmly, I said to Micheal, "Show me the way." Within minutes I had found my flight, I boarded the plane and was off to Cyprus. Once settled on the flight, I asked Micheal why he had not told me earlier where I had to go, and he explained to me that I was too busy to listen. I realized that day something that has stayed with me for years, only in silence could I hear the message, only by becoming still would I be able to move forward.

Finally, I landed at Cyprus airport where my mum was waiting for me, she was happy to see me yet I knew Just by looking at her there was something wrong, even though she was showing me one of her false smiles I knew there was something she was hiding.

I was soon to find out why my mum had not really wanted me to join her in Cyprus. They were living a very poor life. Her husband, although he was a lovely man and he was very kind to me, he had not told the truth about his home in Cyprus, there was no big house and there were no stables with horses, instead the house he lived in I thought was the stable. It was a small house, with the basic essentials not even met. The toilet was a hole in the kitchen floor full of cockroaches and there were many people squeezed into the tiny house.

It was night time when I arrived so I went to bed on arrival. I noticed a little girl in a cot asleep. Yeshim was my new stepsister. I thought it was strange to see a five-year-old girl in a cot but I fell asleep as soon my head hit the pillow.

As I opened my eyes the next morning I was greeted by lots of eyes staring at me, Yeshim and her brother Tolga, along with cousins and neighbour's and any other children in the neighbourhood were all crouched down staring at me. I felt like I was in a zoo.

People were very kind to me in Cyprus but it wasn't long before I began wishing I were at my Nana's eating her cooking.

It was just so poor, not having a toilet was my biggest issue, and I really hated the cockroaches. I made friends with the girl next door, she had a toilet in her house, not a real toilet as I had known all my life, but it was more advanced than the hole in the floor in the kitchen that we had.

Once a week there was a programme on the television that all the children in the neighbourhood would watch. They would come to our house, sit outside on top of an old car, and watch this black and white programme. I would sit there wishing I was at my Nana's, with her huge colour screen television that my mum had bought her and I was watching snooker with my Granddad or Dallas with my Nana, lying on the comfortable sofa and snacking on crisps.

My mum's new in-laws were a lovely old couple who lived in a tin hut and their toilet was at the bottom of the garden, another hole in the floor, this time with chickens running around instead of cockroaches.

My mum did the best for me whilst I was there, but there was really nothing she could do, gone were posh restaurants and fine clothes, life was so basic now that I knew it wouldn't last. I knew my mum would not live this way for much longer, I knew her too well.

One day I went to the park. I was sitting on a swing in the Cyprus heat. I felt so hungry, I had not eaten anything that looked familiar since I had arrived and this day I could hear my tummy crying for food. I started to see all my Nanas cooking in my mind and it made me even hungrier. I noticed the flowers around the park and I jumped off the swing and walked over to a big yellow flower. I could smell its perfume. I knelt down to smell the flowers perfume and that is when the idea came to me.

Within minutes, I had eaten the flower and the one next to it. Suddenly I felt better and I carried on playing.

That night I became ill. I was violently sick and spots had appeared all over my body. After a trip to what seemed like a war hospital and having to confess to my mum that I had eaten flowers in the park it was confirmed, the flower eating was not a good idea. I had an allergic reaction to them. The next day I was booked on the flight back home. My mum followed shortly after.

I was around nine when my mum took me to some psychic fairs in the UK. This was to be a huge influence on me as a child. I felt like I was in magic land. I loved everything I was seeing, the smells, the people and more than anything, the Tarot cards. Each Tarot reader had his or her own deck of cards. It was the first time I saw Tarot cards in detail. It was whilst I was wandering around one of these fairs whilst my mum was having a Tarot reading I met a man who was a Tarot reader there. He looked almost hippie with long hair and a short beard. I started bombarding him with questions and begging him to give me a reading. Of course, I was too young and he refused to read for me. However, he did put his hand on my head. Then he said to me.

"One day you are going to be a great Tarot reader, also, you will be a great medium, you will help many people."

A medium? I was ecstatic about becoming a great Tarot reader. Although I wondered, what he meant about me being a medium. My next quest was to find out what a medium was.

I was to find out a medium is someone who talks to the dead. I remember thinking. I do that all the time. How boring. I thought it was such an easy thing to talk to the dead that it sounded boring. I focused on what he said about me being a great Tarot reader one day. The thought of me owning my own pack of colourful Tarot cards made me that happiest little girl in the world.

We were living in London at the time, since our return from Cyprus life had become very hard for us financially. My mum was working long hours again. My stepsister Yeshim, who had also returned to England, and I would sit in the horrible flat we were living in waiting for my mum's return each night. My mum's marriage was breaking down, her husband was a lovely man and a good man, but the marriage was not working. The financial stress and our living conditions did not help. Yeshim and I ate rice or rice soup for weeks.

Thankfully, as always, help was on its way. My mum and I were returning to Manchester to see my Nana and Granddad. We were sitting on the coach, and as the coach was pulling out of the station, it stopped to let somebody else on. We couldn't see the door of the coach but suddenly my mum turned to me and said, "That's your uncle Donald." I looked at her confused, why would my uncle Donald be in London, why would he be getting on this couch and how did she know that? Suddenly up the stairs of the coach walked my mum's brother, my uncle Donald!

I was so happy to see him, I loved him so much, we had always been so close, but because my mum and I had moved around so much we had lost contact. Two important things came out of that chance meeting, firstly it appeared he lived just around the corner from us in London now, after our return from Manchester I saw him and his wife to be, my aunty Maxine almost every day. Although he and Maxine were not on a great income themselves, I remember the bags of food they would buy for us. Gone was the rice soup. Finally, we were able to eat good meals again.

I love them both very much, my uncle Donald had been in many ways like a dad to me. He would take me sledging in the winter snow and swimming in rivers in the summer. He had always loved me very much and he was such a kind and patient person with me. I always felt loved and safe with him. He always seemed to have all the time in the world for me, treating me like his own daughter.

The second thing that always intrigues me about the coach incident is how my mum knew it was her brother without being able to see anyone, how had she know something before she had seen it? I started to watch my mum closely and it seemed she did seem to "know" many things before they happened.

It was some time later my Granddad took ill. He was losing a lot of weight and the whispers between my family members were the word "cancer." One day I asked Micheal, "What's wrong with my Granddad?" "He's dying," was the reply. I ran upstairs to see my Granddad who was laying on his back in bed. He was thin and frail. He was wearing blue and white pyjamas and his white hair and pale face shocked me on first seeing him. He could not talk. I had not realized he was so sick because I had not been allowed to see him since his returned from the hospital. I ran up to him and hugged him. He kept pointing to the ceiling. I asked him if he was hungry and he nodded his head. I ran back downstairs telling my Nana to give him some food, as he was hungry. My Nana told me he would not eat it. "He will do," I cried. "He said he was hungry." He was so thin I did not understand why they were not feeding him. My Nana gently told me he was dying.

The night my Granddad died, I had a very vivid dream that his coffin was on a bus. A big red, old English bus. I got onto the bus, walked over to his coffin. I then saw his socks, his trousers, his shirt, and then his face. However, it was not my Granddad I was looking at; instead, it was my own dad. I saw the entire episode in slow motion. I stood there looking at his dead body in my dream, on waking I knew that the next death was going to be that of my dad's, I knew it would not be long. I also knew there was nothing I could do about it. My dad was going to die. I could not do anything about it. I don't know how I knew this but at the time, I was convinced of it.

Shortly After my Granddad's death, my mum, my aunty Janet, and my cousin Helen and I all took my Nana to Spain. I loved my cousin Helen and was excited about going away on holiday with her. My mum was separating from her husband at the time so the break appeared to be a good idea for her also. We were booked on a cheap weeklong coach trip to a town called Blanes in the Costa Brava. I couldn't wait to get away from the flat in London. By now I had lived in so many different places, different towns and had been to so many different schools I had lost count. I would often go back and forth to my Nana's house to wherever my mum was living at the time. I do not believe I ever stayed anywhere more than a few months. I moved around so much that even now as an adult, I wake up many mornings and I don't know where I am. It will take me a while for me to realize what country, what town, and then the memory of what house I am in will slowly return to me.

In Spain, I felt for the first time in my life I fitted in. It felt almost like home. It was a feeling I had never experienced before. The town we went to I felt like I knew it already. I went to the beach and felt like I had swum in that same sea all my life. Each time I looked up into the sky from Spain it felt like electricity was going through me. I loved the Spanish language and the Spanish food. Suddenly we had an abundance of food again and I realized I had never tasted anything like Spanish food.

My mum asked me if I was enjoying myself. I told her I was having the time of my life, how much I really liked Spain. My mum was the black sheep of the family. She did more or less as she wanted. She went against all traditional family ways. She smoked, she drank, she had fun, she partied and enjoyed life. She was constantly on the move, and for all these things people would look down their nose at her. We would often be very poor and within days, we would be rich, then a change would happen and we would become very poor again, just surviving on the basics.

However, to me she was the best mum, she always taught me to trust in God and to follow my heart, something that I feel is the best gift any mother can give her child. I have grown up feeling very loved in my life.

As our weeklong holiday finally ended, I stood on my own outside our holiday apartment on the balcony. I stood there and looked up to the deep blue sky, there was not a single cloud around, and I asked aloud to whoever was listening to me. "Please find a way for me to come and live here, this is my home, this is where I want to live." After my plea, I felt a strange feeling of peace and I let out a deep breath as a feeling of trust just came over me, I knew my wish would soon to be granted.

The moment my mum and I were alone after we arrived back to England, she came to me very seriously and told me that the man who owned the bar where we had been going every evening in Spain had offered her a job. How would I feel about moving out to Spain? Needless to say, I did not unpack!

A week later, we were back in Spain, this time, to live and to start yet another adventure.

Chapter 3

Sun, Sea and Psychic

Back in Spain, I had never felt happier in my life. I was born again in the sense that I learnt to talk another language, all the food was a new taste to me, and even simple things like potatoes brought about a completely new experience of herbs and spices I had never tasted before. The way of life was so different. The stars at night shone brighter, the people used hand movements to talk and raised their voices almost as if shouting. Cars appeared the wrong way around and the Spanish drive on the opposite side of the road from the English. Young teenagers all had motorbikes; police officers would join in with the crowd for a drink and a chat. The Spanish were very friendly with me and very soon I felt like I was part of the town, I would be randomly stopped in the street by people wishing me a good day. Each day brought about new and exciting experiences and I loved it. The town itself was a seaside town with miles of beaches, the seafront was alive with bars and Spanish cafes, where both local Spanish and the holidaymakers would sit on the large terraces drinking coffee, or enjoying their meals, often tables were abundant with Spanish tapas.

The town centre itself was a maze of shops, it was always busy, shops opened until very late in the summer time, and it was always full of activity except siesta time when all shops shut during the day so the locals could eat and sleep. I would often walk to the large harbour and watch the fishermen returning from sea with their daily catch, from there I could take a boat trip to neighbouring towns.

Overlooking the town is "San Juan," a mountain, where hidden away was the famous botanical gardens, flowers and plants from all over the world. I would often take a walk up to the old "castle," or take a bus ride up to the top of the mountain. The views from the mountain overlooking Blanes were, and still are breathtakingly beautiful. Often I would pinch myself and wonder how I had come from a small flat in London to paradise.

Around a year after moving to Spain, I was almost eleven and I was sitting on a train from Blanes to Barcelona, a journey that was going to take over an hour. I was alone and was very excited. This was it, I was going to buy my first pack of Tarot cards. I had heard they sold them in Barcelona. Therefore, Barcelona I was going. I got off the train at the Plaza de Cataluña and walked down the famous Rambla. It was a very hot day and with my excitement, I felt like I was about to melt in the heat of the sun. I did not know exactly where they sold Tarot cards, yet the first shop I walked into sold them. I had walked into the shop as though it had been calling me. I bought the only deck on sale and returned back home on the train. The moment I got home, I slowly opened the box. It was a powerful moment for me. I removed them and inspected them one by one. I more or less understood the minor cards, because of my poker card readings. However, the majors were new to me. I had waited all these years and now I held my very first pack of Tarot cards. I remembered what the Tarot reader hippie at the psychic fair had said to me. Could I really be a good Tarot reader? I wondered. I also remembered the bit about me being a medium. How pointless was being a medium compared to the excitement of my colourful Tarot cards?

I almost lived in the bar where my mum worked. My life was bars, swimming pools and the beach, Meals out and sleeping until late. I loved my life. I would spend hours watching the night stars. I would sit and watch sunsets. I would lie back on the beach and stare into the deep blue sky in amazement of its beauty. I would watch the sea for so long, the reflections from the sunlight flickering across the deep blue sea. Everywhere I looked, I seemed to be in paradise. Although I was very aware it was not quite like "The Place." I would often visit in my dreams I was still able to appreciate the beauty around me. I always felt nature was the heart of life.

Life seemed slower in Spain. Days seemed to last forever. Moments seemed to stop in time and last for hours; when I relaxed, I would often find myself in "The Place." It was happening more frequently, I never intended this to happen. I would relax and just find myself in a place of pure peace and beauty. I remember one day sitting on a small wall at the beach. I had been sitting for quite some time and a full moon slowly appeared, it seemed to become bigger and bigger until It appeared so close and so huge I felt I could almost touch it. I could not believe the moon could be so close to me and I was so in awe of its presence, a huge silver disk was metres away from me. I was just about to reach out my hand to see if I could really touch it when suddenly my view changed. I was still sat on the wall by the sea, but everything seemed duller, the moon was now a distant circle millions of miles away, I knew I had just had a change of place, I just knew that for a moment I had gone to "The Place." These episodes started happening to me quite frequently. Spontaneously I would find my surroundings change and I was no longer where I had been, instead, I was in another place. Somehow, I was no longer being transported in my mind to "The Place," instead, it seemed my surroundings were changing and "The Place," was transforming into my surroundings.

In the bar, I started doing Tarot readings for clients, holidaymakers as I had once been. Strange looking back how many people let such a young girl give them a Tarot reading.

My intuition became very strong, and the next few years I began working in the bar and my intuition started showing. I would serve drinks for customers who had not ordered them yet. As I gave people their drinks, they would say, "How did you know that, I haven't ordered it yet?" I would often make a laugh out of it. One time there was a man who walked into the bar, I made him Pernod with lemonade, as I passed it to him and charged him he looked at me and asked how I knew what he drank. "Intuition," I casually replied. He was not impressed. In fact, he believed his wife had put detectives on him whilst he was on holiday. He had never been in the bar before, he had just arrived in Spain, yet I had served him before he had ordered. Now, what would be more possible, the young girl behind the bar is intuitive or that his wife had sent detectives out to spy on him and somehow told the detectives to tell the young girl behind the bar what he drinks? That was the first experience I had with people not wanting to believe in any kind of psychic ability, instead preferring the more complicated version.

It was not just simple things like drinks either. I would know things about people before they told me. I just seemed to know things. I also knew many things that were happening in the world before they happened. I would watch the news in the bar and think. I know all this. People would tell me stories and I would think. I know that already. I started to play with my psychic abilities. I didn't have much else to do with it. I started to guess how many meals we would sell that evening. What time the bar would shut, what dish would sell the most, just little games. I would freely offer Tarot readings to anyone who was interested, surprised by the amount of people who were eager for a reading from me. However, during my readings, I would tell people things that later I would wonder to myself how I had known. I knew intimate details about random people. One lady I gave a reading for was shocked when I told her that she was on her honeymoon, after marrying her ex-husband's brother. She was a little embarrassed and quite surprised as to how I knew; she nor her husband had told anybody about their personal circumstances. "What card says that?" She asked me whilst inspecting my Tarot cards. "Urmm well none," was the only reply I could muster up.

"So how did you know?" She asked with what appeared genuine curiosity. I honestly didn't know how I knew. I just knew things, and when I was giving a Tarot reading, I would know more things. Somewhere within me, I was starting to realize it wasn't the Tarot cards that had magical powers and were giving me information about people, but I just couldn't quite work out what was happening. Either way, I was enjoying giving readings and having positive feedback. I often thought about the old lady on my Nana's road, maybe I could have magical powers like she did.

Chapter 4

The Gentle Giant

At thirteen, I went back to England to stay with my Nana for a holiday. It was mid-march and it was nice to see the greenery of England again. The coldness of March did not seem to bother me. I decided to go to the local park I used to go to often as a child. I sat on a bench smelling the dampness of the trees, when suddenly my view changed. I looked around me and saw the bluest sky I had ever seen, the greenest grass I had ever imagined, and the trees around me seemed to be alive with energy. I could see what appeared to be small whirlwinds of energy swirling around me. I noticed there were many people around me, I could see them clearly, yet at the same time, they seemed transparent whilst transmitting lights of colour. I sat for a while enjoying the bright sunlight and the feeling of peace that was engulfing me. I lost all concept of time. Eventually, I stood up and on standing my entire surroundings changed again.

I realized I was standing in the rain, it was dull, the sky was thick with a blanket of grey clouds, it was almost night time, and I was alone in the park. I knew I had gone to "The Place," or maybe "The Place" had come to me. I ran to my Nana's home to shelter myself from the rain and the coming storm and got into a bit of trouble when I returned late and wet. Clearly, I could not tell my Nana I was late because I had been in an entirely different place other than the local park.

Whilst I was staying at my Nana's, I went to see my dad who was living around the corner from her. It was a Thursday and he was happy to see me. I rarely saw him, only on holidays and now I lived in Spain it was not very often. Still he was my dad. My dad knew everyone, he had friends all over town He was a very tall man and he was known as the gentle giant by many people. I felt I did not really know him as a person. As a child, I had always been so naughty when I visited him because I had wanted his attention. I desperately tried everything to get his attention. I would tell him I was running away and walk out of his house. I was so young and not allowed to cross the road alone. I would hide behind the bushes and watch his front door with anticipation, waiting for him to come looking for me. I did this many times and never once did his front door open. Never did he come looking for me. Eventually, it would start getting cold and dark, I would quietly return to his home, and there was never any mention of my running away. Because I was constantly moving around so much I did not see him very often so when I did see him I desperately wanted his love and my tantrums were really a cry out to him.

Many times when I was a child, he would make a date to come, pick me up, and take me somewhere. I would put my coat on and sit at the bottom of my Nana's stairs waiting, and waiting. "He will come for me this time," I protested to my Nana who often told me to take my coat off, telling me he wouldn't come for me. I cannot remember how many times I fell asleep at the bottom of my Nana's stairs after hours of waiting and he never showed up. Yet this time, it was unlike any other visit. We talked a lot those next few days, we spent each day of that week together. At last, we were like father and daughter. We sat and watched films together and passed the time enjoying each other's company.

I had completely forgotten the dream I had when my Granddad had died about my dad and his dead body and after all, he was only 34 and seemed healthy with no indication of any problems of ill health. He promised to take me to the park the next day for an Easter fair that was on in the area and we were going to spend the entire day together. He was going to pick me up at 9 am. I was doubtful of his promise and I told him I was not sure if I believed him, reminding him about all the times he had let me down. However, this time, he promised me. I eventually took his word for it. He knew he would be in big trouble if he did not come for me.

As I was leaving, he asked me for a kiss. I was standing outside and as a thirteen-year-old; I got all embarrassed about kissing my dad.

"Come on, you're never too old to give your dad a kiss," he said smiling at me. I walked back up the path and gave him a peck. As I walked off again, I looked back at him and he waved to me. He was standing at the doorway, smiling as he watched me leave. I smiled back at him and waved.

I could hear the doorbell ringing. I dived out of bed and looked at my watch. It was nine o'clock. Now I am in trouble, I thought to myself, realizing my dad had come for me and I was still in bed. I reached for my clothes and began to get dressed as quickly as possible. I heard my Nana open the door, "But what do you want?" I heard her ask. Alarm bells rang inside my head, I knew instantly something was wrong. I ran down the stairs wondering why she was asking my dad what he wanted and why she did not just let him in the house whilst he waited for me. The further down the stairs I stepped the more I could see that the man standing at the door was not my dad, instead it was his brother. As I reached the bottom step, I heard my uncle's words. My dad was dead. He was 34 years old and had died of a heart attack.

I could hear screaming. The screams echoed along the street. They appeared to become louder and louder and for a moment, I wondered who was screaming so loud. I then realized it was my own screams. I knew this was going to happen. I knew it when my Granddad had died and I had seen it in my dream. I had known this was going to happen, yet I had done nothing to stop his death.

It took me a long time to accept my dad was dead. All my childhood trying to get his attention, his love, and now he was gone.

Was it cruel of fate for me to have been with him every day that week? We became closer only to have him drop dead on me. He had promised to take me to the park. Instead, he had left for good. Or was it a blessing that I had been there, would I have felt worse if I had not seen him for over a year and I received a phone call whilst I was in Spain informing me that he was dead?. The last memories just a blurry goodbye. Instead, my last memory is a kiss and a feeling of knowing my dad.

Too many questions were invading my thoughts, I just wanted to get back home to Spain. First, I had to attend my dad's funeral. He was catholic and the tradition is to bring the body home. I was shocked when I saw him, not only because of his dead body but because it was exactly as I had seen it in my dream the night my Granddad died, the same socks, same clothes, same haircut, even the same coffin. I looked at his body in slow motion, just as I did in my dream some years earlier.

Consumed with guilt, I wondered if I had explained to him about my dream could I have stopped him from dying. I felt somehow his death was my fault and as I saw his family grieving, I began to feel almost like I had killed him myself.

I spent the next few nights sleeping in the living room and sitting beside his coffin until finally, they took him away. I remember there was a very special moment when the atmosphere suddenly changed. An empty feeling suddenly entered the room. Just as I was feeling the change in the atmosphere, somebody cried out loud, "Brian has gone now," and everyone commented on the change in the room.

Everyone agreed he had now gone. I knew he had gone before then. I had sat with his dead body for two days and nights, so I was sure he was already gone. However, I do feel the change in atmosphere was him leaving the room after sitting with us and going back home to the Spirit world.

My cousin Luke was a young musician and around the same age as me. I feel he did my dad and all the family proud when he played a favourite song of my dad's on his saxophone at the funeral. It was an extremely emotional moment for every person who attended. I looked around and felt quite sad as I realized that I hardly knew anyone at his funeral, I was probably the one person who knew my dad the least. It saddened me so much to think I would never again see him nor would I ever find his love.

The first lines of the funeral song hit me so harsh I felt an overwhelming feeling of grief like I had never felt before "Oceans Apart Day After Day," Richard Marc's "Right Here Waiting For You" song lyrics made me wonder. Was it me he thought of when he heard that song? With me being in Spain and him in England, was I the one that came to his mind as he enjoyed his favourite song? I chose to believe it was for me and he had always loved me and missed me. Now he was, "right there waiting for me."

After the funeral, I really wanted to get back home to Spain. When I arrived, I was able to relax and I reflected upon past events. I wondered where he was, was he watching me? I had seen dead people just walking around, why could I not see him?. I had heard dead people talk to me, so why could I not hear him? Although I understood the basics about death, I needed to know more. I wanted to know where he was, what he was doing and I wanted to know if I understood death to a small point then why was it hurting me so much? I cried so many tears and sometimes I felt a pain in my chest never felt before, a pain of loss. I was confused with myself, my fish had died, my dog had died, and my Granddad had died. I thought death was nothing at all. So why all this pain? Moreover, what was a medium anyway?

The next few years I worked and played in Spain. I enjoyed every day of my life to the maximum, watching the sunset, staring at the stars for hours, swimming in the sea with the fish, taking in all the marvellous views that surrounded me. In between playing with nature and working in a bar, although I was only young and some may say I should have been at school. However, I was learning from life itself. I also managed to read anything I could get my hands on regarding Tarot and the occult, and more so, life after death. Nothing filled the gap my dad had left and although I knew he was in the Spirit world, I wondered why I could not see him. Why was I seeing random dead people and talking to my friendly Spirits yet nothing from my own dad?

It was whilst I was sat watching the TV one day when unexpectedly I started to feel strange. I was hot and cold at the same time and a sickly feeling came over me. I then felt someone was sitting next to me. I slowly turned to see who was at my side and I saw my dad. He smiled at me and disappeared. The entire incident lasted only minutes but it was the first time I had seen my dad since his death.

Some weeks later, he came to me in a dream, a vision so clear and vivid. We were standing outside an old house, the grass surrounding us was uncut, and the garden was overgrown. The Place itself seemed familiar, the air was just as clear as the air in "The Place," yet I knew I had never been to this house before. He had a big dog with him and the dog was playing in the garden. He told me that I would not see him again for a while because he had to spend some time on his home and garden. He told me I would not see him for thirteen years. He hugged me and I kissed him. I told him I loved him. I did not want to let go of him, yet he insisted he had to leave me. "I love you," he said to me and I cried in his arms, as finally I believed him. I looked around and told him that the place where we were looked familiar and the more I looked the more I started to recognize things, the trees seemed to be alive, the sky was crystal clear, the air was transparent, the smell of the flowers was intense, I realized I was in "The Place." My dad must have known what I was thinking as he then told me it was the Afterlife.

I felt like in a way I had always known "The Place" I went to in my dreams or wander into was the Afterlife or Heaven as many people call it but I was happy to have it confirmed for me by my own dad.

On waking my pillow was soaked wet with tears, my face was red and my eyes were puffy. It was thirteen years later until I had my next dream of my dad or any feeling of him around me. Thirteen years later I started to dream of him and now I feel his presence around me often. I did not understand at the time of the dream as to why my dad was going to do gardening. Since then I learnt that some Spirits have issues they choose to work on, I feel my dad chose to work on his issues for a while.

Chapter 5

Psychic Stalker

When I was seventeen, I was still working in the same bar when a Spanish man named Andres came in for a drink. I accidentally knocked a full glass of whisky and coke over him and had to apologise and hand him a towel. That same night I had a very vivid dream of Andres and I just knew on waking I was going to marry him.

Shortly after my eighteenth birthday, we were married. We went to England for a short stay and he liked it so much we ended up staying there for some years. Leaving Spain was like leaving my heart apart from me. However, I know now that my time back in England was part of my path.

At first, I tried the normal more traditional English way of life. I had children, and made cakes. I owned a carpet and had the comfort of a lovely home and garden, but I felt like an alien in a hamster cage. I pushed my psychic side of me away. Placing it in a box of something to do in the future.

However, I was still dreaming every night and with both of my pregnancies, my intuition was at its fullest. Whilst heavily pregnant, I had a dream where I saw a baby girl floating in mid-air towards me. A beautiful perfect girl with jet-black hair. I saw her clearly, she looked familiar as she floated closer and closer to me. She then disappeared into my stomach. I woke up in labour and 18 agonizing hours later (by the way no one ever told me childbirth was like pooping out a watermelon) I had the very same little girl I had seen in my dream, the same face, the same hair, it was the baby from my dream. My Nicole had come into this world. Holding her in my arms brought about an indescribable feeling of pure love like I had never known before.

When I was pregnant with my son I had an almost identical experience, I was dreaming and I saw him floating into me, I saw him just as clearly as you can see a real baby, only there was a blue light surrounding him. Again, I woke up in labour, and now I knew that pooping out a watermelon was not going to rip me to pieces, just an hour and a half later, my Danny was born. He immediately started going blue, the midwife took him off me and cleaned out his airways. After the midwife slapped him and she placed him into my arms, the same child I had seen just a few hours earlier in my dream, again I felt that indescribable feeling of pure love.

I loved being a young mother. However, I was no longer happy being in England. Still I tried to make the most of it. I made a few friends and it was whilst I was with my friend Kerry one day we saw a poster for a psychic development class. We decided to join, for some reason, I had no confidence in myself in England. I thought it would be something fun we could do together. Maybe I would take the psychic side of me out of the box I had shelved it onto; maybe it was time to rekindle my old flame for my Tarot cards.

I was very excited joining the classes; it had been a while since I even picked up a book on the topic. My time had become all about babies and learning to cook.

Linda Clark was the woman who ran the spiritual development group, a tall slim, middle-aged woman who wore her long brown curly hair tied back. I was nervous as I arrived at Linda's small bungalow. Wind chimes were blowing in the wind and creating music as me and Kerry walked up the garden path. I was happy Kerry was with me or I feel I wouldn't have gone. On entering the bungalow, the smell of lavender wafted through the air. Linda showed us into her living room, a circle of chairs had been placed around the room and I noticed there were around ten chairs. I took the chair furthest away from the door. Other women started to arrive and Linda introduced us to each other. Everyone seemed like a friendly bunch.

Linda introduced herself to the group and explained what kind of topics we were going to engage in over the coming months, topics I had read about but had never tried, psychometry, healing, flower reading, using the pendulum. I was excited as I realized there was to be one Tarot week a month. After the introduction, Linda suggested we do a meditation. I felt a burst of excitement. This was it, after being a wife, a mother, a cook, and a cleaner I was now returning to my spiritual path. The big psychic was going to turn on her light.

Only I didn't turn on any light, instead, during the meditation, I felt an intense pain in my head. I can only describe it as a belt being tied around my forehead and being pulled tighter and tighter. Because of the pain, I was unable to do the meditation. Afterwards, Linda asked each person in the group how their meditation had been and most had some wonderful answers. When I told her what had happened to me she smiled at me and said, "That was most likely your third eye." I almost laughed aloud. "What?" I asked, although I feel by the look on my face, she decided not to mention it to me again.

Later on in the evening, we were explained briefly about psychometry, holding an object and connecting to its energy. It sounded fun and I was paired with a tall woman with short hair who gave me her ring for me to hold. I held the ring almost to the point of melting, yet I did not feel anything. Linda had asked us to "feel" if the ring felt hot or cold, if it had a strong or weak energy, did I feel happy or sad holding the ring. I felt nothing. I just felt like I was holding a ring. I heard Linda say to another woman in the group if any images entered her head, then she was to express what she was seeing, as it may be a link. On hearing Linda, I saw an image in my head of a budgie. "I can see a budgie," I blurted out without thinking. The tall woman excitedly replied, "I have a budgie." I was amazed by my own super powers so I continued; "I can see a budgie in a large cage in a large room." The woman looked disappointed for me and quietly said, "No, my budgie is in a small cage on my balcony." I returned her ring and produced my own piece of gold to allow her to try her abilities at melting it.

I was disappointed in myself and rather confused, I wondered why I had not just stopped when she had agreed with my vision. It bothered me I had seen an image of something that was not true. Other than my own disappointment in myself, I had enjoyed the evening and was looking forward to the following week.

When I arrived home, Andres asked me if I had enjoyed my evening, "Yes, I saw a budgie in my head," I replied. He looked at me with a slightly amused look on his face. "But it was in the wrong cage and the wrong place," I said very solemnly. I know he mumbled something but I did not quite catch what.

Although I had not been using my psychic ability's for a while and my Tarot cards were still in a box somewhere, yet I was still visiting the Afterlife often. Sometimes whilst dreaming and sometimes spontaneous visits. I was still dreaming vivid dreams every night and I spoke daily to Micheal and saw Spirits around me.

Although I had an entire lifetime of "strange" experiences, yet, at the same time this course felt different, I felt like I was starting at the beginning. For some odd reason, I did not connect my own experiences with the psychic development course. Looking back, I can see I was using my intuition more than I had realized. I remember one morning that I had woken from a strange dream and for some unknown reason, I asked Andres not to go into work that day. Normally I would not have been happy about him taking the day off, as we needed the money. However, this day I was insistent that he should stay home. He wasn't feeling too well as it happened and he did not take much convincing and after taking some medication he returned to bed.

The following day we were told the work van that Andres travelled to work in each day had been involved in an accident on the motorway. Andre's work colleagues had been covered in industrial cleaning acid that had been in the back of the van. Everyone was in the hospital with injuries. I put it down to luck, but I knew it was not luck. I knew I had dreamed something bad would happen that day and that is why I insisted he stayed home. My uncle Donald would have gone with him that day also, because he and Andres worked together. Thankfully, he didn't go either. In an ideal world, I would have seen the entire picture, including where the accident was to take place and prevent it from happening. However, life was not so simple.

Sometime after joining the course, Linda Clark explained to us about Spirit guides, apparently we all had a guide, a spiritual being that came with us at birth and walks our entire path with us, guiding us, the title says it all, a guide. I thought about this for a while. I just was not sure how much I believed we had a guide, it sounded very fairy tale to me. Yet in the coming months everyone around me seemed to be connecting with their guides, week after week, women in the group would come in and excitingly tell us how they "met" their guide.

After a while, I felt that I had better get one of these guides also. I did not want to miss all the advancements I was seeing in those who had found their guides. Linda had shown us how to find our guide through meditation. At home, I had a room I had created as my spiritual room. Andres had painted it lilac and I had Angel statues placed on my shelves, Angel pictures on the wall, and my crystals lay on my table next to my Tarot cards that I had now removed from storage, it was beautiful. My music player always had dolphin music and sounds of nature playing and I was constantly burning incense. Everyone who entered my room commented on how lovely it was.

For some reason I now found it hard to meditate, I would sit in my room, close my eyes, and end up thinking about dinner or my children. I had been meditating all my life, yet now I found it a pain. I hated having to watch my breathing, I had always breathed and now trying to take deep breaths and concentrate on my breathing seemed harder than it sounded, it would often give me slight panic attacks. The few times I was able to meditate, I found it boring. I had followed the instructions as everyone else in the group had yet their meditations were full of adventure and spiritual awakenings. I seemed to be side tracked. I knew I had to force myself, if not I would never find my guide.

It bothered me that I was unable to meditate, yet often when I was relaxed, whilst in the bath or in bed or sitting in the garden, I would close my eyes and I would find myself floating away, my mind would go to wonderful places. Sometimes I would wander into the Afterlife, other times I would return to Spain and walk down my old street, I would smell the pine trees that lined the street. I would walk along the seafront and just gaze at the sea as I had done many times whilst I lived there. Sometimes my mind floated to a place I had never been before, it was not the Afterlife, Nevertheless, I enjoyed my wandering.

I remember one day, very fed up with myself, I asked Micheal why I could not meditate. I told him quite desperately, if I did not learn how to meditate, I would never find my guide. I remember him laughing at me, no reply other than his laughter.

What was wrong with him lately? I wondered to myself. I had noticed he seemed to be amused with me, just when I needed his answers the most he had stopped talking to me the way he always had and instead would just smile or laugh at me.

Finally, I focused and forced myself enough to do a few meditations. I really wanted to meet my guide and I wondered what kind of guide I had, maybe an Angel like one of the women in the group did or maybe it was a very advanced spiritual soul and when I finally met him or her, they would teach me how to be a great psychic and a wise soul. However, obviously, Micheal wanted to play with me, for some reason he kept entering my meditations, on seeing him I would pull myself out and ask him why he kept doing this to me, again he just smiled at me.

After this happened a few times, I banned Micheal from my meditations.

Although I was advancing in other ways, I had a new deck of Tarot cards, the ancestral path Tarot by Julia watts, a deck of cards I fell in love with at first sight, a deck that spoke to me. Yet I was way behind the others in the group. I had not found my guide, I had not seen any Angels with feathered wings, and I could not even finish a basic meditation. Still, with all the tears and tantrums I enjoyed every moment of it.

The women in the group would often talk about their newfound guides. I would listen and wonder where mine was. "I feel I can tell him anything," I heard a woman say. "I'm sure mine plays games with me," another woman stated with a smile.

"To be honest, I think I have always known mine," one of the quietest women in the group added. The more I listened a thought started to creep into my mind but before the thought was able to form, I brushed it aside and lost it.

Sometime later, I was able to do a meditation. I was on the top of a mountain, and I looked down and could see land below me. I stood right at the very end of the mountain and I jumped yet instead of falling, I began to fly. I felt as free as a bird as I flew through the air. I turned and saw Micheal flying beside me. Instead of leaving my meditation this time, instead, I landed on another mountain top and asked him why he was following me in my meditation, how was I ever going to find my guide if he kept following me?. He just smiled at me and in that instant, I remembered how he was my closest friend, how he had been by my side since I was born and how much he had guided me over the years. I felt completely stupid as I realized he was my guide, he was as good as it gets.

After that meditation, I cried for days, I was an emotional wreck. Everything just seemed to make sense to me. For the next few months I treated him differently, almost like royalty coming for tea, I was careful about what I said to him. I was on my very best spiritual behaviour. I also felt watched and was conscious of him being near me. I started to use words like love and light and wore crystals around my neck and I prayed to the Angels for world peace. I felt like I was in a spiritual greenhouse, I knew Micheal could see everything I did, said and even thought, and now I knew him as my guide it kind of freaked me out.

I joined many other spiritual groups including a meditation group. I was looking forward to the evening as I arrived at the small house. A tall blond haired man opened the door to me. He took me into his very small living room where there were several women sitting on chairs. I sat in the only available chair and gave a nervous smile. I noticed there was a healing bed in the centre of the room and I thought that a little strange. The blond man briefly introduced himself and then he looked at me intensely and said very loudly, "OK, come on do your stuff," and indicated for me to stand in the centre of the room. I turned bright red with embarrassment and nervously asked him, "What stuff?" He leaped out of his chair, stood in the middle of the room and stated "I will have to do it myself, as always," he shook his head from side to side as if he was upset he had to now stand centre stage. Actually, I am not sure exactly what he did that day.

He asked one of the women in the room to lie on the healing bed and claimed he was going to carry out a psychic operation on her. He then began to do the most bizarre things in the air with his hands, claiming to be curing the lady from all illnesses. "I feel something is wrong inside your stomach," he diagnosed for her as he did an operation to fix it. I almost laughed when the woman claimed she did actually feel a bit uncomfortable due to a pie she had eaten before leaving the house. I felt the whole thing was a shambles and after his "show," whilst the women were brushing his ego, he asked me if I would be returning the next week, in all my love and light I told him thank you very much but no, I wouldn't be returning.

On my return home I felt quite upset about the entire evening, I had either witnessed a miracle and brushed it off or I had just been subject to somebody else's spiritual scam. I wasn't comfortable with either option. I felt Micheal come close to me as I sat in my own sorrow. He explained to me that I had to see all sides of the spiritual path. Micheal and I talked as we always did and before I reached my home, we had become the friends we had always been.

My first reading in my lilac room at home was an exciting day for me. Before the reading I spent some time in meditation, I protected myself, opened my third eye, and balanced my chakras. I then cleansed my precious stones whilst I played my dolphin music and lit my incense. My first reading was a young girl named Heidi, she was around my age, and I felt very comfortable with her. I proceeded to give her what I felt was a very good and constructive reading. As the reading ended, I heard the name Dave shouted down my ear by Spirit. "Who's Dave?" I asked. Heidi started crying and through sobs she said, "It's my Granddad."

I knew her Granddad was in the room, I could feel his presence next to me, yet I wasn't sure what to do next. "Well, I feel he is here, most likely just to let you know he is fine and still with you," I told her. Heidi was so happy with those few minutes at the end of the reading that I knew instantly the entire Tarot reading would be forgotten and she would only remember those last few minutes. On leaving, Heidi smiled and looked at me intensely and said, "I didn't know you were a medium." I was surprised by her words, "Nor did I," I replied.

I thought about this for a while after she left. Was I a medium? I had seen dead people all my life, I spoke, felt, heard, and even smelt Spirit. However, it was always random Spirits I encountered, I had no control over who I saw or when. To be a medium I needed to be able to communicate with Spirit in a way to enable me to pass on messages. I had no control over my encounters, just random meetings and messages. However, I realized that more than anything I now wanted to be a medium.

For the next year, I became a psychic stalker, any advert, meeting or group with the name medium, psychic or spiritual in the title, I was there. I started to go to the spiritual churches, I had been a few times with my aunty Maxine when I had first arrived back in

England, but I had only gone out of curiosity, now I went to observe. I watched all the mediums who stood up on stage and observed how they worked. Luckily, it seemed almost every night there was something happening in my area in which I was able to participate.

After some time, I understood what Micheal had meant when he said I was to see all sides to the spiritual path. He meant the way people reacted to certain things. I sure met some strange people. I met the ego seeker, the money makers and the deluded. I also met some who really believed in their own truths. I left the possibility open that maybe their truth was real, if it was not real; it certainly was to them anyway.

Of course, I also had some amazing experiences with very wise souls and I had many magical moments of laughter. I was a regular at most events by this time, observing from the outside yet joining in when invited. I got an invite to join the Spiritual National Union, everyone was joining so I put my name down, filled in a form, and paid my money. I was quite pleased with myself the following week when I received a card stating I was now a provisional member. The woman who had arranged for me to join asked a few others and me if we would like to go to the Arthur Finley College. I was not sure what was at the college, but it sounded spiritual so I paid my fees and headed off.

The Arthur Finley College at Stansted in Essex is one of the most amazing buildings I have ever had the pleasure to visit in the UK. A spiritual school almost without words to describe. Each room was busy with different spiritual activities, different teachers giving talks and demonstrations. I walked into a large hall and watched the medium's do demonstrations. One medium was only a young lad around my age. I wondered how he had come so far so young. I went into another room and Bill Nedderman, a well-known hypnotist was giving a speech about his work. I listened to him for a while and pondered on the idea of past life regression.

I strolled outside to the large, very well kept garden. I sat with a group of people who were all giving and receiving healing. The college was truly amazing and I enjoyed every moment of it.

Some months later, I went to my local spiritualist hall and Bill Nedderman was appearing that night to give a demonstration. I wore a yellow suit that I thought made me look good at the time, I realize now I looked like a canary, yet I believe it was due to the suit and its colour that Bill picked me out of the audience to do a demonstration on me. I was going to be hypnotized.

I wondered if he would be able to hypnotise me because I knew I had such a strong mind. "Do you see this stone?" he asked me. He showed me a stone, I saw it for maybe a second and I was gone, I mean gone. So much for my strong mind!

I was no longer aware of the hall nor those who attended the demonstration, I wasn't even aware of who I was. I had been taken back in time. I could hear Bill asking me questions and I was answering him, yet at the same time, I was standing over a large sink washing clothes. I was in a kitchen with a big open fire. It was a small house and it was obvious I was poor. Under hypnosis, I gave details about my life, my address, and family names, even where my dad worked. I really felt like I was the woman standing at the sink. At one point in the demonstration, I felt a fly on my nose, as I raised my hand up to flick it away I came back from hypnosis. The entire episode had been interesting.

Shortly after, Linda Clark was organizing a Tarot night in a local building she hired out and she asked my friend Kerry and me if we would like to attend and give readings along with other Tarot readers. Boy was I excited! I bought a boring grey suit that I believed made me look respectable, I had my hair cut in a way no one noticed and bought a pair of really ugly shoes.

On arrival at the building, each Tarot reader was given a table to set up in any way we chose. I had taken some of my precious crystals and an Angel statue. I had forgotten my incense but that was fine, within minutes a fellow Tarot reader gave me sacred incense from India. That night I gave nine Tarot readings, I also had some lovely Spirit communication. When I arrived home I was elated, finally, I felt like I was reaching my dreams of becoming a Tarot reader.

I was receiving quite a lot of bookings at home for readings and although I never advertised my services, word of mouth was spreading fast and each day I was receiving more requests for bookings. It was a very exciting time for me as all kinds of people with varied backgrounds were turning up at my home for a reading from me. My friend Kerry lived next door to me and we were able to talk Tarot and talk Spirit, often sharing our learning process on how to communicate with Spirit. The more readings I gave the more practice I received and I was slowly but surely starting to see a pattern in the way I worked as a reader. More importantly, I started to realize that Spirit, although expressed in a variety of ways, Spirit had the same repeated message for me to pass onto their loved ones, and the message was simple. They were still around.

Chapter 6

The Puzzle

The question of how I became a medium is one I am asked often. In a way I could say I was born as a medium, if you consider seeing and hearing Spirit as being a medium. On the other hand, I guess I became a medium due to years of study and practice. It has not always been easy either way I look at it. Seeing random Spirits or the search for Spirit for communication has been equally as emotionally hard.

Although I have seen, felt and heard Spirit since I was a child, Spirit don't just come and talk to me, instead, they communicate in many ways.

Spirit is the energy inside a person. Spirit is an energy that can never die nor dissolve. Their physical bodies are gone but the energy within them is very much alive, so to communicate they use their mind. They reach my own mind and a majority of communication is really happening from one mind to another. Their energies are also so much quicker than mine are. They have no physical bodies to slow them down. They communicate with me using their own energy and mine. Often they will try to do it so quickly that I know I miss half of the information they are sending me, I then have to try to slow my own energy down to be able to become still enough to listen.

The biggest way I learnt they communicated with me was through feeling. I just had a feeling inside me to say something or to express the feeling. This is called clairsentience and it is what I use the most. I don't always have a Spirit tell me they are somebody's Grandma, I just feel it, and no other feeling feels right. I can give an entire reading just by feeling what I have to say. It's the strongest sense I have.

Then I have an image sense, where I see images in my mind. If you close your eyes and visualize your own bedroom, you can see it clearly, you can see where your bed is, what colour the curtains are, where your window is placed, and yet you are seeing it all inside your mind, not with your physical eyes. That's what I learnt to do. Images would just pop into my head. This was one of the hardest things to learn as sometimes I was shown an entire image to state one thing, I may be shown and entire bedroom, but it was only the bed that I was meant to express.

Then there is the physical eye where I have physically seen a Spirit as clear as I was seeing a living person, often only for a few seconds. I believe this is because Spirit doesn't have the energy to express themselves in their former body for too long. Remember Spirit no longer hold onto their living bodies, so they have to project it from their own energy. It takes a lot of energy to do this, and as of yet I haven't worked out how they actually do it.

Spirit, having no physical body also have no vocal cords. Therefore, it's easier for them to transmit their verbal message into my mind. I learnt to listen to them in my mind's ear. I could hear them only inside my head, much like when we talk to ourselves, often their messages are clear and I can pass on a message almost word for word. I noticed that to make it easier for me, the messages always came to me in my own language. Foreign Spirits spoke to me in my own language, later when I returned to Spain they must have felt my Spanish was good enough, as the messages started to come to me in Spanish. Although I do believe Spirit talk in a universal language, if they choose to.

Again, they can sometimes take tremendous energy and speak to me in an audio voice. It's loud and clear but it's often just one word. More often than not it's a name that I hear. Although I appreciate Spirit shouting a name in my ear, at the same time there's not much I can often do with just that one piece of information. "I'm being told the name John," I may say but then I have to use my other senses to work out why I was told the name John.

Sometimes Spirit sends me smells, it's one of my least favourite senses as I am not very good distinguishing smells and I also find they are not very helpful. "Your Grandma always wore channel number five," would be a great piece of information. However, unfortunately, my sense of smell is so bad I would only say, "I smell something sweet, or strong that your Grandma used to wear." That isn't good information, so I do try to avoid smells, although sometimes in a reading I have had my client smell something they themselves connected with very strongly, for example, whilst communicating with the Grandma I have had the client say, "I can smell channel number 5 so strongly and that's what my Grandma used to always wear." I think maybe Spirit gave up on me and smells, so instead now send them directly to my client.

Only on occasion has having the ability to smell whilst working with Spirit been helpful for me. Once, I was giving a reading for a man and his father had come through in Spirit. I was overwhelmed with the smell of rubber burning and yet my client couldn't smell anything. When I told him I couldn't quite work out how his father had died as all I was receiving was the smell of burning, my client told me his father had died electrocuted whilst at work and the smell of burning had lingered in the workplace for weeks.

Physical illness is one of the first things I learnt to communicate with Spirit. Until I described what I was feeling I often feel the illness of what the Spirit died from. I will feel sick with cancer or a shooting pain go up my arm and into my chest with a heart attack. I will feel a strong pain in my head with a brain tumour or a sudden impact of an accident. It often lasts for only minutes and it's obviously not an agonising pain, but it just gives me enough information to know how the Spirit died. I often wondered why they showed me how they died. Most people don't need reminding of how their loved ones died, but I later learnt by Spirit that their death was their last physical experience so to those living loved ones it is an important part of their being. Although Spirit has shown me many times how their own death means nothing to them, only those who are living suffer from the memory of the death of a loved one.

Spirit communication is basically all about decoding messages. It's not a one on one conversation. Unless they show me something, no matter how they chose to show it me, but unless they show me something I cannot feel, hear, smell nor see it. They have to show it to me by some means. Sometimes they throw me so much information I only catch half of it, and sometimes they show me important pieces of information but leave out great details because they just assume my client knows it. A reading is much like a huge puzzle that I have to piece together in my own mind and find the words to pass on a message. Complicated? Extremely!

The hardest part about learning to communicate with Spirit was learning to trust myself. It's easy to want more, it's easy to say more than what I am actually receiving. It's even easier to make a mistake in what I am feeling and say something that is completely wrong. The truth has a ring to it. Just try telling a lie and inside you can just feel that it's not right. Sometimes I will decode an image I am seeing and as soon as I've said it I knew it wasn't right. Therefore, I have to then decode it again. I have to say what I am feeling and it has to be true, if not it just doesn't feel right inside. Sometimes the entire process can be a huge disappointment. Once, I was seeing a lady in my mind and the thing that struck me most about the image was the dress she was wearing, it looked handmade, "Your sister was a designer," I blurted out. "No, she wasn't," was the reply. So then I asked if she was into fashion, again I got told no, so finally I explained what I was seeing, I was seeing a blue dress that looked handmade and had little embroidery emblems on it. The sister then forgave my errors and told me that was the dress her sister was buried in. Sometimes what I am seeing is literally all I am supposed to say.

Another time I had a mother come to me who it came to light that her son had passed into Spirit. In my mind's eye, I was seeing James Dean on his motorbike. "Did your son die in a bike accident?" I asked, "No," was the reply.

"I am seeing a bike, did he own a bike?" again I was told no. I told her other information I was receiving and the mother could understand the messages, but I couldn't get James Dean out of my head, my mind was working ten to a dozen, "Did your son like acting?" again, "No," was the reply.

I began feeling embarrassed. Now I had heard her say no three times, and I still had no idea what Spirit was trying to show me. As the mother was leaving, she spoke a bit about her son. "We called him James, after my favourite actor James Dean, he used to love that fact, and he was as much of a fan as I was," she told me as she left. I felt like kicking myself. There was no point me telling her now that

James Dean was what I was really supposed to have said, having got so many things wrong the last thing she needed was for me to tell her, "That's what I was going to say." I felt so disappointed and frustrated at myself, why hadn't I just told her what I had been shown.

Incidents like this happen, Spirit shows me something hoping that I will say the right thing and sometimes I go completely off track and say everything other than what it is they are actually showing me. There is nothing clear about a Spirit message. It's just a huge telepathic puzzle, and like a stew I have to receive the right ingredients and place them all together and hope and I don't overdo it, under do it, or mess the entire thing up, but in all my learning and with mistakes, I was doing well with my process.

Almost every Tarot reading I was giving, Spirit would pop through to communicate with their loved ones. Always giving the message that they are still around. I gave readings, one after the other and soon people heard I was a medium. I was enjoying every moment of my readings and learning with each one. Suddenly magic moments were happening all around me. Now anything connected with life after death had taken up all my spare time. Along with being a wife and a mum, I was a medium and I loved each moment of it. I was growing as a medium by the day.

Sometime later Kerry's mum, Dee, joined the psychic development group we had been attending. She had seen our progress and wanted to give it a go herself.

Chapter 7

Follow the Butterfly

I was surprised when Kerry told me her mum wanted to join the spiritual development group we attended. I never really spoke much to Dee as I found that we didn't have much to say to each other. Instead, I feel we tried to avoid each other as much as possible. However, I watched intrigued each week as I began to see changes in Dee.

I had been slightly disappointed when Kerry said her mum was coming to a Native American Pow Wow we had arranged to go to with the group.

A Pow Wow is a gathering of Native American Indians, where the Natives give talks and workshops to join in with and are able to teach about their culture and traditions. The Pow Wow was taking place on a large field near the famous Stonehenge. I was able to see Stonehenge that day and feel the magic energy it expels. I also danced a scarf dance with other visitors and listened to traditional Native music whilst I watched the making of dream catchers.

A Native American Indian man was singing a healing song. I wished I understood a bit more regarding their traditions but still, I stood still and listened to his singing. His voice was very powerful and an energy seemed to take over the entire field. I looked up and saw an eagle fly up above us. I wondered what it would feel like to fly, to fly home to Spain. Briefly, I saw Dee running towards me crying. I jumped out of my thoughts and asked her what was wrong. "Listen to him sing," she cried as she ran past me. I was unsure what had happened and unsure if I should go after her or not. Instead, I stood and listened to him sing as she had instructed. Later I was to learn that the song had brought up many deep-rooted emotions in Dee and she was about to start a journey that would take me with her.

Shortly after the Pow Wow Dee asked me if I would give her a reading, I was very unsure about doing so. However, I agreed to it and I found myself turning up at her house with my Tarot cards in hand.

Dee had a spare room she had turned into her meditation room. I was very impressed with the peaceful energy in the room was and how much effort Dee had put into creating such a calming place. I cannot remember a word of the reading. Nevertheless, I do remember as we finished, Dee confessed to me that she had not liked me when she first met me. She told me that she realized now that she saw me as a reflection of herself. She explained to me how sometimes when we feel we do not like someone it is often because we are looking at a reflection of ourselves that we do not like or do not want to confront in ourselves. Then she hugged me, a real genuine hug. From that moment forward Dee became one of my closest friends, not just Kerry's mum.

Dee had thrown herself into her spiritual journey just as much as I had. She and Kerry went away for a week to a spiritual retreat in Wales. Whilst there, Dee tried trance medium for the first time and enjoyed her experience. On their return, Kerry and Dee decided to start a small weekly group, just the three of us at Dee's house.

The group was much needed for me at the time and sounded like fun. We were going to do a different activity each week, including healing, Tarot, the pendulum and all other psychic activities. We were to start with a meditation and Dee was going to try trance, just as she had whilst in Wales.

I was excited as I arrived at Dee's house that first week. I thought I more or less knew what we were going to be doing. Little did I know that the following six months would have the biggest impact on my spiritual path ever.

Kerry and I were both sat happily on the sofa opposite Dee as she closed her eyes and was about to try trance. The energy in the room was calming yet almost buzzing at the same time. I hoped that the trance worked and a Spirit may even talk through Dee, although I did not expect too much to happen. Dee did not say anything and after some time sitting in silence, I looked around the room. I noticed the room seemed blurry, almost as though it was covered in a mist. I looked back at Dee and saw what I never thought possible. Gradually, I was seeing Dee's face change. I saw her teeth grow, her eyes became wide, her slim face became square and her pale skin was now darker whilst a small stubby beard slowly appeared.

Dee's face changed in front of my eyes to a man who appeared Indian. Both Kerry and I saw the same thing happening. The fear that ran up and down my body was like none I had ever felt before. I wanted this man gone, I wanted Dee back, and I wanted out of that room. Slowly the man disappeared and Dee returned. I dived out of the room and into the kitchen as quickly as possible.

It was only after I felt safe in the bright lights of the kitchen did the reality of what had just happened hit me. Then my curious side got the better of me and I wanted more. We agreed to meet the following week at the same time to see if anything like this could happen again. Our plans for what we were going to do each week had now been forgotten. Instead, I wanted to stare at Dee to see if it could happen again.

The next six months can only be described as phenomenal. I have never heard nor seen anything like it since. Each week Dee would change into a different person. Kerry and I would both describe what we were witnessing. Dee never spoke a word for a long time, she just sat in silence whilst Kerry and I witnessed her disappear as Spirits took her place. Other phenomena also happened in the group. Both Kerry and I were touched by Spirit, we saw what we later found out to be orbs, like round balls of light that some people see in photos. We also saw stars appear, little stars of light that would come and go. Energy would fill the room in the form of mist and often a blue tinted transparent mist that we had no words to describe appeared. We would hear clear knockings and tapping's coming from inside the room.

One memory that sticks out very clear to me was when Kerry and I both sat on Dee's very big old sofa bed. We were both staring at Dee describing what we were seeing, as Dee's face became that of an elderly woman wearing pearl earrings. Suddenly the entire sofa bed lifted into the air. My legs were dangling in mid-air. Kerry let out a scream with the shock of us being lifted in the air whilst I tried to calm her although I was anything but calm myself. Following that week, I never felt any fear of anything that happened around us. I loved each moment of the group. I was conscious of the fact that I was experiencing something that very few other people had experienced. Dee and I also became closer as each week passed and by now, the three of us had become a close group. We were all practical people with no nonsense to what we were seeing. If anything, the opposite were true, often we would hear things that we would dismiss as possible outside, non-Spirit activity.

Six months to the day, Spirit shut the group down, no explanation, and no reason. It was just over. I was devastated at the time and it took me a long time to appreciate the magic I had been lucky to witness. I now believe that Spirit wanted us to taste something that was the extreme of Spirit communication. For me to witness how much Spirit are capable of using their energy to communicate with us in various ways, how Spirit can manifest their energy. I also believe it was for us to have a lifetime experience and for us to create the bond we did. I do not believe it was ever intended to be forever, just a taste of a different side of the Spirit world.

I stopped going to many spiritual places after Dee's group shut down. My experiences in the group had been so big that I felt empty in other groups. I began to question everything more than I had previously. I questioned my own part in the spiritual world. At Dee's group, we would often sing before trance to build up the energy in the room, an idea of Dee's. We sang Vera Lynne, Cliff Richard and Abba songs, and we laughed so much. After the group finished, I wondered if there was any point in my dolphin music and my wind blowing music.

Dee set up a website for us so we could share some of our thoughts. This website was to be an important stepping-stone for my path. That is where I was able to question everything and have feedback from others. People started joining the website and I would ask questions and think for weeks about the replies I received. I questioned everything but really, I was questioning myself.

I started to wonder if I had become a textbook reader. While reading so many books and being in so many groups, was I now doing what I felt right or was I so desperate to be a medium I was following the textbook codes. I decided I did not want to be someone who blindly followed others. The groups I was in were all very much the same.

Somebody on Dee's website started a thread about cherry picking, which meant only picking the cherries you wanted on your spiritual path. This thread, as many others, had a huge impact on me. Was I cherry picking? Lighting incense before a reading because it was the right thing to do, even if I did not like the smell. Playing annoying dolphin music because it was what all other Tarot readers did. Placing articles around me that I had very little understanding about, simply because they looked spiritual. Was I the Tarot reader I dreamt of becoming? Was I the medium I wanted to be? I realized I was off balance on my spiritual path. I decided to move away, I moved closer to my mum, this time, my Angel statues, and the mind numbing music was not coming with me.

I moved to a place right next to the sea and yet in the country, a lovely part of England where my mind could enjoy nature, I started to do as I pleased. I meditated to any music I liked, it was up to me. I studied subjects more to their roots, not just the glossy parts. I did readings in my kitchen, with dinner cooking instead of the smell of incense. I found freedom in my path. I stopped being a textbook Tarot reader and medium and instead went with what I felt. It was a moment of growing up spiritually for me.

I missed Dee and Kerry terribly, but Kerry often came to visit me and I spoke to Dee regularly on the Internet. I was constantly on her website asking and replying. Her site became my home and Dee became my living guide. Dee had written her own life story on the site, something that I know had been very hard for her. She had told her own story about the death of her mother when she was just five, her lifelong battle with PMT, and her roller coaster ride of depression. As she wrote each word of her past, her emotions would flow from her. I thought it was very brave of her to do something so publicly yet so personal. I admired her deeply.

On the site, we all knew Dee as the butterfly or the dragonfly, her role often changed depending on her current feelings. It was others on the site that saw her like this and gave her these names. Every time I saw a butterfly, I knew an important message had been left on the website, and I couldn't wait to run home and get online. Butterflies and dragonflies started to become a part of my life. Dee was passing onto me, and others, all her spiritual knowledge that she was learning. In a short period of time Dee had become very strong spiritually and very wise.

Dee was writing a thread on her website that lasted three days. I did not really understand it at the time. There was a part of the thread about her choosing what door to go through. It was shortly after her posting the last thread Dee had a massive heart attack. My husband drove me to the hospital as quickly as the motorway would allow him to drive.

The next three days were sad yet magical. I knew many of Dee's family by now, so on arrival at the hospital, I was welcomed and immediately felt like part of the family. Standing around the hospital bed, her children each read out loud chapters of her own journey, her own life, in her own words. Dee was in a vegetable state, it was heart breaking. I brushed her hair and sang the songs we used to sing in the group. I whispered how much I loved her in her ear. We all spoke constantly to her, even though she was unconscious, we knew she could hear us. We all knew her Spirit could hear us.

We stayed by her side night and day. Those three days seemed like weeks, with little magical moments happening all around us. Even at such a tragic time, laughter would echo around the silence of the hospital, it helped us.

On the third day, Dee chose what door she needed to take and in one of those moments when almost everyone just popped out of the hospital room, she left this world for the next.

We had not realized at the time, but Dee had left her funeral wishes on her website. Silly threads had been popping up about what we want if we die and what kind of funeral we want. It was all there in black and white for her family to read. Dee did not want black at her funeral. Instead, she wanted everyone to wear colour. I wore a pink dress, and even the funeral parlour men wore normal clothes. Pinks, purples and blues, it looked like a wedding. I found myself in a tiny church in a pink dress singing the songs we often sang in whilst in our group. "I Believe in Angels," by Abba and Cliff Richard songs. It was a beautiful funeral for a beautiful woman.

I owe so much of my spiritual growth not only to Dee's life but also to her death. Not a day goes by where I do not remember Dee. Her funeral was full of laughter and love, full of magic and wonder. It showed just how much she was able to change her life. In doing so, she changed mine also. I will always be in debt to Dee for all she taught me, not only the spiritual experience but also about human nature. The circle of love I hold so dear will be in my heart forever.

Each time I see a butterfly or a dragonfly, I remember my dear friend, who like a butterfly, gently flew home.

After Dee's passing, I went away with Kerry and her sister Joanne. Joanne is also a good friend and someone who I love dearly. We went back to the spiritual retreat in Wales, where Dee had been to previously and experienced her first taste of trance. It was a fantastic week away in the Welsh valleys. Hafan y Coad is much like paradise in Wales. The people at the spiritual retreat were very friendly. It was a week of healing, trance medium, mediumship, and an entire programme of Spiritual activities. I had a week of fun and learning. Whilst at Hafan I had my first try of doing stand-up medium. To stand in a large hall full of strangers and pick somebody out to pass on Spirit communications was overwhelming to me. I didn't know if any Spirit would present themselves to me, and I honestly didn't know how I would find a voice within me with so many eyes staring at me. Was I scared? No, I was petrified.

When I finally did stand up, I was convinced I was about to fall down with fear. So many people just looking at me. I stood in the middle of the large hall, feeling naked to the world. Suddenly the people just seemed to disappear. In a room full of people, I could only see one man. My nerves disappeared and I stepped closer to this man and said, "I sense your father is in Spirit," He nodded in agreement. I then went on to describe his father and to talk about the kind of man his father was. I also spoke about problems they had between them and the fact that his father had a skin disease. His father then gave me a beautiful message, then he disappeared.

On his departure, the room started to reappear and I saw faces all staring at me again. I was more than happy with myself and with Spirit for making my first experience so easy. I then went on to give out a few more messages before my time was over and another budding medium was to come onto the stage.

It was not long after returning from Hafan, I began my own groups at home. Friends and strangers would come to my house and we would enjoy spending time together and practicing spiritual arts. I was giving plenty of readings and never short of bookings, I was very relaxed in my work now. In a way I felt I had come full circle, I had gone from being a child who saw Spirit and often visited the Spirit world, the Afterlife as my dad called it, to a young mum who had spent many years trying to control my encounters with Spirit and understand the Spirit world. Then to get lost along the way with rules and textbooks only to then return to starting point. Although I had learnt a lot over the years attending courses and groups and all things spiritual. The main thing I had come to understand was that the answers had always been within me.

A friend of mine from Dee's website said I held my own magic. He told me that one day I would find there was no magic, only what I created myself. I remember arguing with him and telling him, I could not create anything. He told me I would realize that all the answers I was searching for were within me all the time. It had been some years since my friend Richard told me that, now I finally understood him.

Chapter 8

Spirits At Home

Spirit activity has always happened around me and the more readings I was giving, the more things started to happen. My husband, who had completely supported me in my quest of Spirit, also started to see Spirits in the house.

At one time, the room where I did my readings was on the ground floor of our three-story house. The room also lead into our back garden. Sometimes my husband would go into my reading room to go through to the back garden and he would see a Spirit or feel a

Spirit. He has a good sense of Spirit smell and would often smell strong perfumes.

Many times before reading was due he would say to me, "There is a Spirit mother coming," and he would describe what he was seeing and feeling. After my reading, I would return upstairs and excitedly explain to him how my client did have a mother who had passed and yes, she did come through and she was just as he had described. I always wanted Andres to take it further, but he always refused.

Once, on entering my reading room, I saw a little blond boy sat on the sofa. I saw him so clearly that I shouted for Andres to see if he could also see him. (Instead of simply asking the boy who he was or what he wanted). Andres came down and I asked him to go and look in my room and tell me if he could see anything. On his return, He told me he could see a little blond boy sitting on my sofa. I was happy that we were both seeing the same Spirit. It gave me encouragement to think that I was not the only one seeing Spirits in my home.

It turned out that the woman I was preparing my room for did not turn up for a reading and another date was set, for some while I had the little blond boy just sitting on my sofa in my room. Finally, I had the lightning idea to ask him what he wanted. He told me he was waiting for someone. Again, the same woman missed her following appointment, and I think she herself felt embarrassed and didn't want to ask me again. Instead, she sent a friend for a reading. She waited outside whilst her friend came into my room for a reading.

I then saw the blond boy again, this time he was smiling. I asked my client if she knew who this boy could be. She did not know him, but she said that her friend who had missed two appointments with me was waiting outside in the car, and that she had known a little blond boy who had died. We brought the friend inside and lovely Spirit communication between the boy and the woman was able to take place. When she left, I never saw the boy again. It amazes me that he had waited weeks to get his message across to this woman, and finally out of patience, he was able to connect with her. How clever are children?

I was happy that Andres was having his own experiences, but wondered why he wouldn't do anything with them, why not learn more, maybe try to do some mediumship or something, but I realize now that it wasn't the path he wanted to take.

From a young age, my children also had spiritual experiences. From the age they could talk, they would share their experience with me. Children have not long come from Spirit so it is easier for them to have Spirit encounters.

Nicole was only young when one morning she climbed into bed with me. I noticed she appeared to be staring at the wall, I told her to close her eyes and go to sleep. "Who's that lady mummy?" she asked.

I looked at the wall and I saw nobody, "What lady?" I asked. She then described to me a woman in detail. She also told me she was floating, "How can she float?" Nicole asked me in amazement.

She got a bit confused and frustrated at me for not being able to see the woman. She could not understand why I could not see the same woman she could. Not wanting to close any doors to a further experience she may have, I told my daughter that this woman was special and sometimes these special people can't be seen by too many people at the same time.

Sometime later, Danny, who is 18 months younger than Nicole, casually told me that he had been having a great time playing on the computer with a man. I asked him what man and he went on to describe my father in law. Later that evening I casually brought out some old photos and sat on the sofa with Danny. Without saying a word I opened each page, when I came to a photo of my father in law, Danny casually said, "That's the man who was playing with me."

He told me that many times he plays the computer with him. It did not surprise me that my father in law had been playing with his grandson. He was a big, fun man from Andalusia and I had a great relationship with him. He was also a very good Granddad, he doted on all his grandchildren. My niece and nephew saw him daily but because we were still living in England, he had only ever seen my children on a couple of holidays we had taken to Spain and Danny was only a baby in arms at the time.

He was a very typical Spanish man, he loved his gazpacho and he would make litres of it, the more garlic the better, he would tell the same stories repeatedly about the time he spent in Gibraltar and he had an opinion about everything, including if Gibraltar is really English or Spanish. My husband was devastated when his father died and again I saw a different kind of grief. To this day, all his family misses him tremendously.

My children also had other experiences. Andres worked early morning shifts and would leave us all fast asleep in bed whilst he went to work. One day after he left, Nicole came into my bedroom and woke me up shouting at me, "Mummy, there's somebody knocking on the door," I looked at the time and thought to myself, there is no way I am opening the door to anybody at this time. I listened for a while and heard nothing. "Mummy you have to get up and go to the door," Nicole insisted. I told her I could not hear anything and there was nobody at the door. She was so persistent that I got up and looked out of the window, "See, there's nobody there," I told her as I fell back into bed. Nicole was now becoming so frustrated with me that I knew there was no chance she would let me go back to sleep unless I went to the door. I put my dressing gown on and decided to open and close the door, prove to her that there was nobody there and finally sleep.

I had to pass Danny's bedroom to reach the front door. I always left his door open and as I passed his room, I just happened to glance at him, it was the scariest sight ever. My son was being strangled by his own sheet! Somehow, his sheet had become tangled and twisted around his neck. Panic stricken, I ran into his bedroom just as he started to change colour. I pulled the sheet from around his tiny neck with all my force. He started to cough and then to cry. Thankfully, he was fine. I know that a few moments longer and the unthinkable would have happened. Of course, there was nobody at the door.

In that same house, we had another important incident that involved my daughter. She was upstairs playing one day when suddenly she stood at the top of the stairs and shouted me. I shouted back up to her from the kitchen. I was just about to light the cooker to start dinner, but she wanted me to come to the stairs. It sounded urgent. I walked out of the kitchen and went to the bottom of the stairs, "What do you want?" I asked. She stared at me blankly, "Nicole why did you shout me, what do you want?" I asked again. She stared blankly at me and I got a funny feeling come all over me. I looked at her and she finally replied to me, "Nothing," as she said it, I heard a small type of bang, like a small explosion. Then a smell of gas appeared and shortly the hallway reeked of gas. I ran up the stairs, grabbed Nicole, grabbed Danny, and grabbed the phone. Within seconds, we were outside in the front garden and as most women do, I phoned for help.

The fire brigade arrived and entered my home. After what seemed like ages, they finally allowed me to re-enter my home. The fireman explained to me that they had not found the problem, but my home was now safe. Confused, I asked what he meant by "they had not found the problem".

The fireman explained to me that my cooker was a huge hazard, in fact, so huge they took it out of my kitchen, put yellow tape around it and cut any pipe that had enabled it to work. "It's for the bin," the fireman said. Then he explained to me that there was a leak in my cooker and gas had built up inside. At some point very soon I was going to light the cooker and my house would blow up.

The only problem was the gas that had built up had no smell, the fireman did not know why I had smelt gas, I had no other gas leak, and it did not make sense, nor did the small bang I had heard, he assured me the cooker blowing up would have been a big bang. They checked my house throughout, but the smell had gone before they had arrived. Nothing else could be done. Left with no cooker and puzzled, I could not work out what had happened.

That evening as I was about to go up the stairs, I noticed something shining on the floor, as I bent down to pick it up I noticed little bits of broken pink plastic, it looked familiar but I couldn't quite work out what it was. Then I realized it was a lighter, it must have been left on the radiator and had blown up with the heat from the radiator, and it was just where I had been standing earlier. Of course, it explained the small bang and the smell of gas.

At first, I felt embarrassed as I realized I had phoned the fire brigade because my lighter blew up. Then I realized that my entire house could have blown up if I had not had phoned them. I thought about how lucky I was and what a coincidence that I went to the stairs at that very moment. I remembered I only went to the stairs because of Nicole, so I asked her why she had shouted me insistently earlier. "Because a voice in my head told me to," she replied.

Incidents like this have happened often with my children. For no apparent reason, they made me do something and it turned out to be for a completely different reason.

Once when I picked my son up from school, he was about six at the time, he looked very sad. I asked him what was wrong. He told me his teacher was yellow and brown. I laughed at his silliness and asked what he meant by yellow and brown. "Those colours that are around people's bodies, you know the colours that come out and shine from outside your body?" "Yes," I replied slowly realizing he was seeing auras as I had also seen as a child. "Well, my teacher is yellow and brown," he stated. Then he changed the subject. The next day the teacher was not at school. She was off for a long time due to illness.

Danny started to state facts casually about things that later happened. He would make comments to me about my friends or things that were happening on the news and later I would find out that his predictions had come true. We all tried not to make a big deal out of it, although it became standard in our family that whenever there was a big decision we were unsure about we would say, "Let's ask Danny."

One day whilst in a restaurant eating a meal I saw Danny look over at me, I knew by his face that something strange was passing through his mind. As if in slow motion, he suddenly fell off his chair. He did not hurt himself. However, he was very serious for the rest of the evening. Later, when we were alone at home, I asked him what the problem was and he told me that he had known he was going to fall off the chair, he saw it happen in his mind a few moments before.

As young as was, he didn't see the point of knowing something was going to happen if he could not prevent it. My own memories of knowing my dad was going to die and not doing anything about it came flooding back to me. I remembered dreams I would have of plane crashes and world disasters and watching the news, the next day feeling helpless as the dream became a reality.

A few weeks later, I was walking into his bedroom when I heard him talking. For a moment, I thought he had a friend with him because I was sure I could hear somebody else with him. However, on opening the door, I realized no other children had come to my house that day. I walked in and caught him in mid-sentence. "Who are you talking to?" I asked looking around. "Just my friend," he replied. I pursued it more, "what friend?" he then went into detail to describe his friend and the game they were playing together. He obviously wanted to dismiss me and continue playing, but I wanted to know more as things like this was happening more often. "Danny, I can't see your friend," I explained to him. I was then to receive a reply that even to me, was like something from a film.

"Yes, I know mum, you never see any of my friends, and I'm not sure why, by the way, I also see your dad all the time and he told me to give you a kiss, you're still not too old."

I almost passed out; I did not expect this message from anyone, especially from my seven-year-old son. I smiled at him and slowly walked out of the room. I went into my bedroom and cried my eyes out. My dad was with me, he had met his grandchildren, and he had sent me a kiss. I realized the power of Spirit communication. I had needed to hear that message at the time. I had never told anyone my dad's last words to me. "You are never too old to have a kiss".

There was another time where my son brought tears to me without realizing it. I had been running a shop, running a disaster. It was the biggest nightmare of my life. My faith pushed to its limits, I felt that I had no way out to see the light. As I closed the shop one night to return home, I looked up and I begged my good friend Dee, who had died some years earlier by now, to please, just give me a sign. I asked her to give me a sign she was with me and I wasn't alone. I needed it so much. I walked home slowly, I was so desperate, and I felt I just needed something to help me realize that I, too, also had Spirits watching out for me, that I was not walking this path alone.

On the way home, I looked around for a sign. I would have taken any sign as a sign from my friend at the time. I was so desperate, even a stop sign in the street would have cheered me up. However, I received nothing. Ok, I thought, well, I know that sometimes it can take a while. I went home and forgot all about it. Later on that evening, my son came running up to me with his hands over his ears. Quite agitated he almost shouted at me "I can't get this song out of my head, there's a stupid song that just keeps going around and around in my head and its driving me nuts and it's horrible," he screamed at me. Confused and amused at the same time as my son ran around like a headless chicken I asked him what this horrid song was? He went on to sing to me, "I have a dream, a song to sing". I went white as I listened to him. We had sung that song at Dee's funeral. After Danny sang parts of the song to me he suddenly took his hands from his ears and declared, "Wow, it's gone now, thank God for that," and disappeared to go and play with his play station as every young boy does. If ever there was a sign for me that was it. I knew there and then that I was not alone and how stupid I had been to think so.

Both my children have had many more experiences, but they started to talk less and less to me about them. As all children do, they started to grow and their daily lives took priority. Yet I have seen first-hand the potential they both have and I know one day in some way they will both find themselves back on this path.

Chapter 9

Sun, Sea and Spirit

It was a warm sunny day in England and my husband was driving the car whilst I was sitting beside him as a happy passenger. I looked up and saw a plane fly above us. I watched the plane as it flew further and further away in the distance. I realized at that moment I would give anything to be on board that flight, flying back home to Spain.

I almost cried as I became conscious of how much I missed Spain. I spoke to my husband about returning, at first, he did not want to leave England and was against the idea of giving up what we had built up over the years to go to nothing. Yet inside it felt like it was the right thing for me to do and I was able to convince him it was time to go home.

A month later, we were sitting on a plane returning to Spain. We had four suitcases, little money and two children. Friends had said I was mad to just leave, but my heart told me I was about to start my next chapter.

Returning to Spain was fantastic, my children started the local Spanish school, they spoke no Spanish and I prayed as I watched them go into class on that first day. My daughter almost crying, as she did not want to start a school where she did not understand the language. I sat on a small wall outside the school the entire day waiting for the end of class bell, praying I had made the right move. I was so relieved when I saw them both leave the building with big smiles on their faces. Within a month, they were both speaking Spanish better than I did.

One concern I had about returning was my readings. Would the Spanish want a reading from an English girl? Did they know what a medium was? Would I be able to find clients? These were my main concerns as a Tarot reader and medium.

I need not have worried, within weeks of moving I had met a friend, a woman I had known briefly some years previous and I told her I was a medium. It felt strange telling her about my readings. I realized for the first time I had left Spain as a young girl who had many spiritual experiences and I had returned as a wife, a mother, and a medium. I gave my friend a reading and the following weeks she would bring me new clients, those clients brought me more clients and within a few months, I had a continuing flow of bookings.

My friend told me about a friend of hers named Beli who was also a Tarot reader, would I like to do a Tarot exchange? I thought about it for a while, I hadn't had a reading for myself for what seemed like years and I was quite excited by the thought of it, so I agreed, something told me this was going to be interesting.

Beli hopped into my home, having just had an operation on her knee. We gave a reading exchange and I realized Beli was a very good Tarot reader who worked much the same way I did, and that day I made a friend for life, it was not a gradual friendship, it was immediate. I was lucky to meet someone who although may not agree with everything I did, she understood me.

The next few years I became bombarded with readings, local people and people from afar would phone me for bookings, Switzerland, Germany, America, Italy, Dubai and Yugoslavia, were just some of the places people were coming from for a reading from me. I felt extremely honoured, as my name seemed to be passed around from person to person. I didn't have to advertise or try to sell my readings, word of mouth was working for me perfectly again.

I was blessed that as I was embarking on my next chapter of my journey, Beli was also on hers, enabling us to spend hours together talking and sharing our experiences, talking Tarot, Spirit and anything else that was happening in our life's at the time.

Yet at the same time, whilst flash cars were parking outside my apartment and I was signing confidentiality papers from clients, clients with so much money that after they left, the smell of money would linger in my reading room for hours, I was still just me. I still had the same bills to pay, children to feed, house to clean. I would often make huge mistakes in my own life. I had no time to allow my ego to take over as I was too busy trying to pay bills and cook meals, I certainly learnt 101 ways to create meals with eggs and potatoes.

People began to stop me in the street and ask me random questions on spiritual subjects, often-bizarre questions. I would try quickly to process all the information I had ever read somehow to find a reply. I was grateful to the hundreds of books I had read and my good memory.

Once whilst in a shop, a woman asked me the meaning of dragons. She wanted to know what did dragons mean symbolically, and why they were important in her life. I remembered a deck of Tarot cards I had bought almost a decade earlier and there had been a mythical connection to them so I had taken some time to study the subject, including dragons. On this particular day, I was tired and for the life of me, I could not remember a thing about the symbolism of a dragon. I tried to come up with some lame answer, but the woman started to interrogate me more on the subject. Finally, I told her I just did not know. She was not impressed with me at all, in fact, she seemed rather angry with me.

During my daily phone call to Beli, I commented to her about the woman and her dragon questions. It had bothered me, not only my lack of memory, but also her bad response to me, especially since all this had taken place whilst I was standing in a shop. Beli just laughed and replied to me, "You can't expect to pretend to know everything." The phone calls with Beli are often my lifeline, as she walks the same spiritual path as me. I am able to tell her everything yet at the same time she is so down to earth. I felt a huge relief come over me as I realized why I was feeling so exhausted. I could not pretend to know everything. I speak to the dead, not to dragons. From that experience, I learnt to simply say, "I don't know," when I did not know the answer to something. Taking the pressure off me trying to know the answers to every question I was asked, meant I could actually concentrate on the things I did know about.

I was able to start a few groups in my home. Friends would come to my house once a week and we would do different Spirit activities. There was a time we were doing some kind of connecting with the Other Side when somebody in the group had become very emotional and had spent some time crying and everyone felt it was a positive thing to allow them to let their emotions flow.

The following week something funny happened, or at least, it appeared funny to Beli and me as we both started laughing, tears were rolling down our cheeks with laughter. We got into trouble for our laughter. Obviously, everyone knew how serious I took my work and how important Spirits are to me, yet still apparently tears are acceptable yet laughter is not? I remembered the magical times whilst in the group with Dee. How we laughed and how our laughter would increase our Spirit activities. Now I was in trouble for laughing and in my own group, in my own home!

Walking around with an incense stick, a bunch of crystals and taking everything so serious, certainly was not my idea of spiritual activity; I had been through that stage of my life. I had enough tears whilst I was giving readings when I would often have to pass on messages from Spirit to their loved ones, often a child the age of my own would come through and pass on a message to the mother, leaving me with a feeling of grief after the reading. I had enough tantrums whilst trying desperately to understand why some things did not work in the way I chose them to work. Why my own loved ones in Spirit would not come to me when I wanted them to, why did they only appear to me in their own time? Now I wanted to enjoy my path, and if something funny happened all the better.

That was not the only time Beli and I were in trouble either, we seemed to get into trouble quite a lot for being ourselves. Each year we would go to a gathering at the beach, a friend of ours would arrange the group, and we would sit on the sand at night time, give thanks to the universe, and make a wish for the following year. This one year on arrival, I noticed some people in the group had brought a bottle of whisky and coke and were enjoying it between two of them. It was a lovely night and everyone seemed to be enjoying themselves until something silly, but funny happened and Beli and I looked at each other and burst out laughing, again being unable to stop our laughter. I honestly did not think it would be much of a problem as we were in a large group at the beach, some were drinking, some were talking, and others were in the sea. Again, we got into trouble for our laughter and I never received an invite again. Obviously, I was not spiritual enough to say thanks by the sea, but the laughter that I shared with Beli was always much needed.

I never regretted moving back to Spain. I enjoyed swimming in the sea with my children on their lunch break, going out at night for a drink, soaking up the summer sun. I even enjoyed the Spanish storms that would occur every now and again. I was lucky to have readings on a daily basis and Spirits were talking to me loud and clear. I was able to ring or meet up with Beli so we could swap experiences. We didn't just laugh, we also had many tears and conversations that would last until the early hours of the morning.

My mum and her husband Rick decided to follow me to Spain and enjoy the life of sun, sea, and sangria. It was shortly after their move when I began having dreams about Rick being ill, in my dreams he was dying. In one dream, I was reading the Tarot cards for him and each card was the death card, all 78 cards were the death card. In another dream, he was returning to the UK because he was ill and was dying, I woke up sobbing.

The dreams began to bother me so much that one day after our morning coffee, I spoke to Rick about my dreams. Rick went very quiet and told me he hadn't been well but he didn't want my mum to know just yet as they had a lot of family members due to fly over for a holiday. I was in a dilemma, do I keep my word and not mention it to my mum or do I tell her, me and my mum are so close and so connected I didn't know how I would possibly keep such a secret from her.

That night I went to bed unsure what to do and I had a feeling of doom, as I knew in my heart that Rick was ill. Fortunately, my mum woke up during the night after also experiencing a bad dream.

She went to the bathroom and saw blood in the toilet, she knew it could only be Rick's blood and the next morning she confronted him about it. Rick told her about the symptoms he was experiencing and shortly after he went to the doctors and eventually they returned to the UK. He had cancer.

It was a heart-wrenching time. To see my mum look after and care for the man she loved and to watch him slowly die was devastating. My mum had always been the bell of the ball, a fun, loving, kind person who always brought a smile to everyone. We are very much alike with the same sense of humour and I have always laughed with my mum. However, Rick's illness took her smile away. I could see how strong she was being and I could see a sadness in her eyes where only laughter had been. My mum had always been a strong person and a spiritual person. Now she was using all her strength with full force. The cancer nurses told me my mum deserved a medal for how well she was looking after Rick. She cared for him each step of the way, not only physically, but also emotionally, keeping him comfortable right up until the end.

It was such a hard time for everyone and for me, not only was I losing my friend but I was also seeing deep into the soul of my mum. Watching somebody else's grief gives a feeling of uselessness. I felt useless, as I was unable to give anything more than empty words.

After Rick's death, my mum returned to Spain to be close to my family and me again. A heart breaking time in our life, an emptiness that followed us all around. It took us a long time to accept he was no longer with us physically. My readings became more personal yet again, every message I passed on to a client from Spirit I would feel the clients grief, or was it my own grief I was feeling?

Nicole took Rick's death very hard. She had loved him like a Granddad. She was very young and it was her first touch with death. Although I worked and lived communicating with Spirit and dealing with grief, I found it hard to comfort or help my own daughter.

Chapter 10

Dead Broke Medium

The question of whether or not a medium should charge for their services is one that has been asked many times and I am always happy to give my own personal thoughts on this.

When I first started to give private readings at my own home, I didn't charge, instead, I accepted voluntary payments or an exchange for my service. I once had a woman bring me a carton of milk in exchange for a reading. In a way, I was just happy to be able to give readings and each one of my early readings became important experiences for me. Sometimes I felt that maybe I should be paying the client as I was learning so much about communicating with Spirit and about my own limits with each reading.

As time passed and my services were becoming more in demand I found my agenda becoming booked up very quickly. My time was stretched between my work, my children, my husband, my home, and my readings. One night I had a reading booked for a woman who turned up at my house with a friend, I ended up giving a reading for them both. During her reading, she phoned another friend who also arrived for a reading and I gave a reading to all three of them, I finished the night around 11 o'clock. When my clients had left, I turned the light off in my reading room and walked into my living room, only to find my husband sitting alone watching the TV and my children fast asleep in bed. It dawned on me that I hadn't seen my children all day and, other than good experience for myself, I had no extra income from it.

The next day I didn't feel like giving any readings, I just no longer felt like giving away any of my time that I could be spending with my family, but I had a reading booked and no way of cancelling. The woman for the booked reading pulled up outside my house in a luxury car. It was a long reading, as she seemed to have a whole list of questions and opinions. She was clearly a very wealthy woman and I was glad when her brother, who had passed over into Spirit came through and gave her some lovely messages. I could see she was uncomfortable with the tears that were rolling down her face, "This is really going to ruin my makeup," she complained to me at one point as she reached into her Gucci bag for a tissue.

I had explained clearly to my client that I didn't charge, but I accepted an exchange. On my table, I had a small string tie bag where clients were welcome to leave any voluntary payment they wished to, much like a tip. When my client left, I reached for my bag and realized it was empty, she had left me nothing.

That night I started to think about how much money it had cost me to create a reading space in my spare room, wallpaper, a table and the chairs, a sofa. I thought about how much money I had spent in the last year attending countless demonstrations and groups. I had been on endless courses and I would often take a bus or a taxi. Not only did I start to calculate the amount of money I had spent but also the endless hours I had spent away from my family. I realized that I was on a low income and had two children to bring up and this wasn't making much sense, no matter how fulfilling it was on a spiritual level, it wasn't working for me.

From that point onwards, I started charging. If someone were to go to a hairdresser or to have a massage, they would be expected to pay, why not if they go to a medium. I was once told that a medium should not charge as they were doing "God's work." I tried to point out that God has many jobs that people do for him in this world and most are paid. Working in care for others is God's work, bringing newborn babies safely into this world is surely God's work. Along with an endless list of jobs. Now, rather than get into a huge debate about whether or not a medium should charge for their services I often end the conversation promptly by explaining that I don't charge for my work, I charge for my time.

Somebody will inevitably bring out the name of a famous medium and say how much they are charging and how terrible it is that they can charge so much. The reply I have is simple. Don't go, if you feel the service of a medium is too much then find a cheaper one or don't go to one. If a medium charges more than another it doesn't mean they are better or worse than another it just means that is the price they have valued their time and/or service.

I have found over the years that people do not become full-time mediums to make quick money, in fact, most mediums will tell you how hard it is to start working as a medium and that until you build steady clients, the financial side of it all can be a nightmare.

I found myself on more than one occasion to be a dead broke medium, working as a medium part time along with my full-time job was just tiresome and there are only so many years one can keep up that kind of rhythm. Working full time as a medium and not having any financial backup is much like jumping into a black hole and depending on your own strength and faith to slowly crawl out. I have done both, worked full time and ran home so I was able to spend the remaining part of my evening giving readings. Many times, I have depended on a reading to be able to run out and buy food so my family could eat. Many times, I have wondered why I am a financial mess when I am doing "God's work." I struggled for years with a fluctuant income and no sick pay.

The roller coaster ride I was on in Spain slowly became one of chaos, my days of swimming with my children in the sea amongst the fish had ended, my days of slow walks to the harbour had stopped, and something started to change. I kept embarking on business adventures that brought financial disaster, at one point I worked two jobs and would rush home to do readings in the evening. The only stability I had were my readings, they were constant. I was never short of people to read for and I was so grateful. In a way it felt like I was leading a double life, I would wake up to the sun and a sea view, enjoy a creamy morning coffee, and then I would rush around working and juggling my jobs with my readings. I would be thrown a life lesson but have to rush home to make the children's dinner. I had to share my time between my business, my job, my readings and my home life. I just didn't feel I had enough time in any given day. I never had a day off and no matter how much I made the same amount would have to be paid out.

I missed the long days, I saw my friends less and less as I was always working or always tired. I no longer participated in any town activity as I never had the time and my desire had died down. The town itself seemed to be dying along with me. I saw many friends move away, I saw bars and restaurants closing down daily, old friends would die or move back to their hometown after a lifetime in my town. Shops were closing down at a fast pace. The town was no longer kept updated and my much-loved promenade had changed.

Yet at the same time, I had to enjoy life with my children. Relax around them, and try my hardest to be the best mum I could. I became unbalanced and I realized I was walking around in big circles. I just wanted peace. Friends kept telling me I should quit all my mundane jobs and business adventures that weren't benefiting me and instead just concentrate on my readings full time. My guide Micheal had told me years ago I would write a book, but I hardly had time to read my mail never mind write a book, plus, I didn't feel I was interesting enough. One thing is my friend Beli being interested enough in me to talk with me for hours but writing a book seemed like such a challenge, I started and stopped a few times. I wrote and deleted over the years, many pages until the messages started to become louder and louder. Time had taught me to trust in Spirit, yet I was scared of relying solely on my readings. I was scared if I found myself without readings how would we eat.

One day I went for a walk along the promenade and I saw a boat pass by on the horizon, I felt overwhelmed, much like when I had seen the plane fly over me all those years ago in the UK. For one moment, everything made sense, just for one moment I realized that my time in my town had come to an end, there was nothing left for me to do there anymore. All doors had been walked through, I realized that my time in that little Spanish town by the sea had ended some time ago, this was why I was now walking around in circles, and I had nowhere else to go other than in a big circle. Unless I broke the circle and left.

However, where was I supposed to go? That answer would come to me in a dream, I dreamt I was in Benidorm, I was working as a full-time medium and I was writing a book.

My mum had asked me to go to Benidorm years previous as she had always like it, but for some reason the times I had been on holiday there it hadn't really appealed to me. I thought that maybe I had dreamt about Benidorm because my mum had been trying to convince me to move there with her. She had moved close to me after Rick's death, but I knew she would have been happier in Benidorm.

My husband, my children and I were sitting outside a bar on a terrace enjoying a morning coffee. The small town church was directly in front of us and the sea behind us. It was very calming and quiet; to make conversation I mentioned my dream of the previous night about Benidorm. I was surprised by everyone's reaction, before I had finished my coffee everyone had agreed it was time to move on, funny how I had thought it was my full circle but hadn't thought that it was also my family's time to move on.

A month later, I found myself in Benidorm. I had yet again given up everything I knew and was now restarting my life.

Chapter 11

The Magic of Spirit

Since the hippy Tarot reader man at the psychic fair told me I would one day become a medium I feel I have fulfilled his prediction. I am also very aware I still have a lot of learning on this journey of bringing the two worlds together. Each day I learn more about my own capabilities and myself. I also learn on a daily basis how Spirits are truly magical and I am in constant wonder at the marvellous ways Spirits are able to bring a message across to those they love.

Learning of the many ways Spirits communicate has been a very colourful time for me. I have marvelled in the magic of Spirit. I have enjoyed rich and famous people come to me for readings along with politicians, musicians, artists, and very successful business people.

I have had days where I have had a reading for a top politician who arrived in a flash car followed by a school cleaner who came to me on the bus, and I have enjoyed each reading equally. Spirit do not care about what you have, they only care about who you truly are.

They see what you hold on the inside, not the title you carry around on the outside.

Spirit has rather placed me in the right place at the right time or they have brought me the people they wanted me to read for. Bringing people to me from all over the world.

I have also had the frustration of my own failings. I have cried buckets of tears from other people's grief, never in front of a client, but alone. I have cried for what seemed like days. I have experienced anger at myself for my failings. I have been stubborn, and sometimes I have not understood the process and have taken my anger out at Spirit, claiming I was never doing this work again. I have screamed at the wind and have cried in anger at my own lack of understanding. Yet I have always been able to pick myself up or to take myself down from my high horse and continue with my path.

I am a hard working medium yet I will admit I am also very lazy in my field. I have turned down a huge amount of opportunities over the years and instead taken on mundane business ventures that are in no way connected to my spiritual work only to then become angry with Spirit because I realized I was on the wrong path. Yet throughout it all, I have always received a continuing flow of readings. Sometimes when I have felt truly lost, I will remember the many readings I have had with magical moments and that is enough to help me to continue. Not every reading is full of Spirit messages with such clear evidence, magic is unlikely to be sprinkled over every reading and this to me can be very frustrating, yet I know that I always do my best.

I often remember a woman named Carmen who came to see me for a reading and a male Spirit friend of hers came through. He was showing me the sea and the harbour. I suddenly felt very cold and I felt like I was gasping for breath. Carmen explained to me that her friend had fallen into the sea at the harbour and he had drowned. He gave some good evidence, but he also told me to remind Carmen she needed to go for a test with her gynecologist. Carmen was very surprised at this reminder from her Spirit friend yet I was even more surprised. I did not want to scare Carmen yet I did not want to brush the information off. I felt very bad when she left after the reading and it bothered me for days, especially since Carmen told me she did not like going to the gynecologist, as it was one of her fears.

She was almost white when she left. I put myself in her shoes and I really felt like I had just scared the poor woman. I did not want people to leave my readings with more problems or fears then when they entered. That was not the reason I was on this journey. I was also very aware of my responsibility as a reader. I have my own code of ethics and that includes sending people to the correct places, go to a financial adviser if you have a financial issue, go to a psychologist if you have a mental issue, and above all go to the doctor if you have a health issue.

It was over six months later when I saw Carmen again. When I saw her, I felt an overwhelming feeling of panic as I remembered her reading. Yet Carmen came running over to me and gave me a big hug and whispered, "Thank you, thank you," repeatedly to me.

Carmen then went on to tell me that she made an appointment with the gynecologist the day after seeing me. She hated them and had no previous plan to do so, but the reading had been so accurate she felt she could not ignore the message. Her results were not good, Carmen had cervical cancer and the doctors told her how very lucky she was to have found it in time. Having no symptoms at all, she would never have made that appointment if it were not for her friend in Spirit who had warned her. She had the operation, the cancer was removed and she is fine now. She was very grateful for the reading and for her Spirit friend. I remember Carmen a lot when I have one of those moments where I feel low about my work.

Not all people I have read for have felt the magic of the reading even with Spirit messages. I had a woman named Beatrice who came for a reading not very long ago. I was reading for over an hour with her and her brother had come through in Spirit with very good clear Spirit messages, he showed me details that really seemed to touch her. When I told her that she had her brothers rosary beads hanging on a picture in her bedroom, she became very emotional and confirmed that she did. She then explained to me the special story behind the rosary beads and why it was of such importance to her that her brother had acknowledged the fact that she had them and how she cherished them.

Her brother spoke a lot to Beatrice and I felt the reading was beautiful with not only her brother but also other family members passing on messages from the Other Side. When the reading was over Beatrice suddenly changed her mind. Claiming that an hour was not long enough and other readers she had been to see had spent at least three hours with her. I felt like every word I had said, every message I had passed on to her, she had just thrown into the bin.

She was not happy with the reading because she wanted more time. I explained to Beatrice that I could no longer feel or connect with the Spirits around her. I had passed on the messages and there was no more I could do. I tried to remind her about how much detail and how many messages she had received yet she was adamant that other readers had spent longer with her.

After Beatrice left, I felt sad and I decided to go home. I really felt that all the messages and proof from Spirit had been for nothing. I felt deflated and wondered if maybe I was the only one who realized how beautiful it was to have our loved ones in Spirit come to communicate with us. On my way home, I saw Beatrice with a group of friends. I was almost behind her when I heard her telling her friends all about her reading with me. She spoke so negatively about the reading I felt physically sick.

She did not mention her brother or her other family members who came from Spirit to give her messages and personal details, she also did not mention how emotional the reading had been for her; how she had asked me for tissues as her tears fell. Instead, I heard her say, "I was only in for around an hour," and three times, she declared, "The last one I went to I was in for over three hours."

It is not the first time I have felt deflated after giving a reading. Once I had a woman who had fantastic evidence from her husband and her father from Spirit. The evidence was so clear even I was quite impressed. Her husband gave me the date of their wedding anniversary and her birth date, Spirit doesn't often give me dates. Her father told me that she kept his reading glasses on her chest of drawers in her bedroom and they had been lost for a few months.

The woman was very happy and confirmed all the details that had come through in the reading. It was only after the reading I was to find out that she had been highly disappointed with me because her mother had not connected to me. She was sure that any good medium would have picked up on her mother who had passed some years earlier and they had been very close. Her high expectations of who she felt I should connect to meant that the messages she did receive were cast aside and instead of being happy, she was disappointed with me.

Trust in what I am feeling has been the hardest lesson for me in my work, although it was a Dutch woman who was my ultimate proof that what I felt from Spirit was what I should trust in. The Dutch woman was a police officer. Throughout the reading, she had contact with her loved ones who were now passed and it was at the point when I felt her aunt in Spirit that the Dutch woman looked at me blankly and said, "No, I don't have an aunt in Spirit." I really felt I was right with what I was feeling so I continued, "An aunt who passed with cancer," again I heard, "No," I felt more information come through, "Your aunt who passed with cancer and never had children," again, I heard the Dutch police officer very clearly say, "No." I was slightly nervous inside but for some reason, I had to trust the information I was receiving. I knew if I did not follow my instinct that day I would never be strong enough to understand the messages I was receiving. If a client said no and I backed away, I would never understand why I receive some information. "Your aunt who passed with cancer, who never had children and loved you like a child," I continued, again I heard a clear "No." I was very frustrated with myself yet I needed to understand why I was receiving incorrect information, I felt sorry for the Dutch policewoman as she must have felt frustrated also. Suddenly I heard more information, "She died in Amsterdam," I said. On hearing my words, the police officer jumped up from her chair. There was a moment of commotion as she instantly realized who I was talking about. She began to cry, "I can't believe I forgot about my dear aunt, she was like a mother to me." Suddenly she had remembered her aunt, who died of cancer, had no children, loved her like a daughter and had died in Amsterdam. For me, it was a moment of relief. As the Dutch woman cried whilst remembering her much-loved aunty and almost kicking herself for not remembering somebody who had been so important to her, I realized that this to me was a huge learning point about trusting Spirit and the information I was receiving.

Since the reading with the Dutch woman, I have been surprised at how many people seem to briefly forget about their loved ones. I have seen it happen so many times I have lost count.

Another puzzling experience that happens regularly is like in the case of a woman who I felt her brother had passed from a heart attack. I heard my client, much like the Dutch woman, say to me "No," repeatedly. The brother kept giving me more and more information, some information was quite clear. I almost gave up, but I knew I had to find out who this Spirit man was who was claiming to be my client's brother. So eventually, I took a deep breath and I asked her outright. "Do you have a brother who passed with a heart attack?" I asked. I was slightly confused and exhausted by this point. Her reply shocked me, "Yes, I do have a brother in the Spirit world, and yes he did die of a heart attack, but it can't be him." Immediately and with genuine curiosity, I asked her, "Why not?" her reply has echoed over the decades with so many other clients. "Because he died years ago." I took a deep breath and calmly replied to her, "Well, he's still dead."

So many times since then I have heard the same thing repeated to me. I feel some people genuinely must think there is some type of time limit on the length of time you can be dead, or somehow Spirits who passed over a long time ago are no longer allowed to come through with a message.

There has also been a lot of frustration with me where I have had to pass a message on to somebody from the Spirit world, but I have come across as a complete fraud until the bigger picture was understood. Like with a woman named Marie who during a reading I suddenly felt the presence of a young boy. Marie didn't know a young boy who had passed, but I felt she was strongly connected to the young boy's mother. Marie denied any knowledge of knowing a mother whose young son had passed. I felt the young boy's illness had been a long illness and he had died in hospital. Again, Marie came to a blank. I could tell she was really trying to cooperate with me, but no matter how much she thought about it, she could not think of anyone she knew who had lost a young boy due to illness. I felt deflated as I apologized to Marie and to make me look even worse, I even passed a message onto Marie. I told her that she did know the mother and that soon she would see her and to tell her that her son was fine on the Other Side. He was no longer in pain and he was still by his mother's side whenever she needed him.

To say I felt bad when Marie left would be an understatement. Not only had I insisted she knew somebody she was adamant she didn't know, I even went as far to give her a message. I would not have blamed Marie at all if she had not left my home that day believing I was nothing more than a fraud.

Some days later, whilst Marie was ironing that she suddenly remembered a friend of hers who had lost her son. Marie hadn't thought about this friend only because the friend had lost her son before Marie had known her. For some reason, she didn't connect her friend to the boy whilst at my house. Marie did see the boys mum a few days later and she had the courage to pass on the message.

Marie became responsible for many more readings I had and for many spiritual reunions.

Spirits work in many ways and one day whilst at work Marie met a man who was holding a book under his arm. Marie was reading the same book at the time. After a general conversation, Marie gave him my number and suggested he come to see me. His name was Juanjo and since our first meeting his own journey has also changed directions and Juanjo is now helping many people on the spiritual path.

The first time he told me, "It's all about love, love is everything," I thought he might have lost the plot slightly and gone over the edge into crazy land. Like everything in my life, I had to find out for myself that in fact, the simple message Juanjo wanted me to understand was actually the truest lesson.

From journeying into the Afterlife to being lifted in the air whilst sitting on a sofa bed, from giving messages from Spirit to bringing comfort to their loved ones, to seeing dead people. All the magic that has happened to me over the years, the pure magic of Spirit that has been bewildering and illuminating, the very simple message Spirit have shown me is that it is all about love.

Spirit love, they don't judge, they don't hate, they don't want nor do they need. They just love.

I believe that is what they want from us; they want us to live in a world of love, to love others and to be loved back. I don't need to try to imagine a world based on love as I have been there, in the Afterlife. There is one message I hear repeatedly from Spirit, I believe they say it to try to bring comfort and peace to their loved ones, it's a message that I myself have needed to hear many times and have felt a sense of peace when passing it on. That whether it be a loved one who has passed over or a loved one you have not met in this lifetime, you are loved enough to have someone always by your side.

Part Two

In Between Worlds

Chapter 12

Heaven Is So Close

Where is the Spirit world, or where is Heaven? Is a question I am asked a lot.

First, it is important to understand that before we started this journey of life we were spiritual beings living a very active Spirit life. We enjoyed a full, happy life in the afterlife and loved ones from all our previous lives surrounded us. In the Spirit world, there is an order, a system for everything. The physical life is a reflection of the wonderful, magical Spirit world.

Before a medicine is invented to save lives, before an idea is realized that will improve humanity, it has already been created in the Spirit world.

In the Afterlife, all Spirits work hard on their own evolution and for the well-being of the physical world. Spirits can also take on any appearance they choose and are able to speak a universal language of thought.

At some point, we decided to return to the physical world. There are a number of reasons we may decide to return. It may be because we feel we want to learn something, or to experience something that we were unable to experience on our previous visits to the physical world. Or, it may be the reason for returning is not for our own benefit, but instead to help a loved one in some way who has already returned to this world. Maybe our return is to benefit humanity by returning to the physical world to create something that will improve or save lives. There are multiple layers of reasons as to why we choose to return to the physical world.

Throughout our lifetimes, we stay within our spiritual family. All people we meet in this lifetime are people we were connected to in some way in a previous existence. Somebody from our Spirit family will decide not to return this time with us, but instead to guide us from the spiritual realm in the best way they can. My friend Micheal was the one who decided not to return again this time, but instead to stay in Spirit to help guide me in this lifetime.

The entire process is worked on before our return whilst still in the Spirit world. Where we will be born, into what family, who will be our parents this time? Every important question is asked and our destiny will be entwined with the destinies of others with the hope we accomplish our true reasons for returning. Having a true destiny, a reason for our being and knowing that we ourselves created our very own destiny before we were even born is sometimes the hardest thing to understand in life, especially for those who have suffered terrible heartaches and desperation in life. Yet, as hard as it may seem to believe, I do believe that we have the life we do because we chose to live that moment.

Of course, in life, we can never see the bigger picture. We can never understand how our suffering may bring a cure to stop all further suffering. Our poverty may bring about a world where there is no more poverty. One action, one word, one thought, one idea can all bring about world change and create a better future for all future generations, most of us will become our very own future generations.

There is an understanding of the Spirit world and a system that seems so hard to comprehend whilst in the physical world, but I know our destinies are part of our own planned out future.

Of course, although our destiny is mapped out and certain points are stopping points we will reach. We still have free will. At any given moment, we can take the road that we choose to take on. We can drive any car we choose or take a plane, we can stop and get lost for a while, we may even choose to go backwards sometimes, and many of us choose to stop and sit on the sideline for many years. That is free will. Our soul knows our true potential and our guide knows our true reason for our being. However, our conscience mind has forgotten, it's ironic to know that our own free will is the only thing that can stop us from reaching our true destiny.

When we die

When we pass over from our living world back home to our spiritual world, our physical body breaks down and our Spirit leaves our body from the crown of our head. Our feet being the first place our Spirit leaves our physical body.

It makes no difference how long it takes our physical body to die our Spirit will start remembering our true home. For some of us our memories may return slowly as we are dying with a long illness, for others who pass suddenly our memories may return almost instantly.

As our Spirit leaves our body, it goes directly to the Spirit world. It makes no difference how we die or if we were good or bad. Each and every one of us will return home when we die.

When we die we don't go to Heaven where there is an old man sat at the gate waiting to give permission of entry. The Spirit world is so close to our world that I feel it almost overlaps, there seems to be no distance to the spiritual world; it is almost as if it's a thought away. It's a space that is just outside ours. There is no long travelling to reach the Spirit world. The two worlds are so close I believe they touch.

On arrival, a family member or friend will greet us and will then lead us to our huge spiritual families, we will meet up with all those we have loved and passed before us.

As our memories return, we start to remember how the Spirit world works, how we lived before our journey to the physical world.

The reunion we encounter with our love ones is a huge celebration for us and for all our Spirit family.

Yet immediately we are able to see the physical world. We can see our loved ones who are still alive and are crying for us, we can feel their pain, their grief for us. At any moment, we can be by their side, not physically but our energy can.

We are suddenly able to live in both worlds, we can stand next to our living loved ones, we can feel their feelings, we can whisper in their ears. Yet at the same time, we can feel the glory of the Spirit world.

Most Spirits attend their own funerals; they stand with their loved ones. From the moment Spirits pass over they are able to join us when they chose to, with just one thought they are by our sides.

They are able to enjoy the wonders of the world of Spirit and at the same time, they are able to enjoy the beauty of our physical world in its purest form. They cannot touch a tree, but they can hear its music, they can feel its pulse, they can smell its fragrance from miles away, and they can see colours in a way they could never have imagined when alive.

A green field of grass, viewed by Spirit is a spectrum of colours with the aura of each colour shining our far beyond every stem of grass, it's alive with sound and movement, its colours are vibrating and the smells are like perfume that we could never bottle in the physical world.

Everything in the Spirit world is amplified, everything is bigger. The aura of every flower, every plant, every rock and stem of grass is dancing around, all things bringing a dance of music, colour and smell.

In the living world, we can see only a much-dimmed reflection of what we can see in nature from Spirits eyes. The Spirit world is not a physical place, it is another dimension. It's a parallel world to ours. It's a place where thought is everything. We can create anything, just by thinking about it, we can be anywhere within seconds. No planes to catch, no tickets to pay for. Just thinking of a place we can instantly be there.

We can also reproduce anything we choose to in the Afterlife. We can go for a walk with our loved ones who are in Spirit and sit and eat an ice cream. Not a physical ice cream but one that is created in our minds, enjoyed in our Spirit. Not only is it limitless, it's free and we don't have to worry about our weight.

The Spirit world is truly a magical world where thought creates anything we choose. In our physical world, we are now starting very slowly to realize the power of our minds. How our thoughts can create our environment and how we can create a better future. We are just touching slightly on the knowledge of what Spirit knows and how they live.

Thankfully, as we adapt to the Spirit world again our material thinking leaves us, all negative thoughts we had whilst living no longer exist. Only love and joy can exist in the Spirit world. Jealousy, greed, and all nasty thoughts are unable to enter our minds whilst in the Spirit world. Instead, fun, laughter, kindness and peace are just some of the wonderful feelings we are constantly feeling as Spirit.

The easiest way to explain where the Spirit world is would be to explain it as Spirit explained it to me.

"The Spirit world is like your next door neighbours, we are right next door. Anytime you need us just call us, just think of us and we will be with you in seconds, we don't live with you, but we are right by your side, always keeping an eye on what you are doing and how your life is going, yet never intruding or overstaying."

Judgment day

Sometime, the Spirit world doesn't have time like we do so it would be hard to say how long, however, Sometime after we return home to the spiritual world, we have to have our own judgment day.

As living beings, we send out a ripple effect in life, each and everything we do at some point affects somebody else. There are simple actions we do without knowledge of the effect, like not shopping in a certain shop because we don't like the owner and advising others not to. The owner some years later goes bankrupt and takes their own life, by this time we have no interest in this shopkeeper and may never know the effect we left or how we somehow participated in his downfall. Then there is intentional badness such as raping, stealing, abusing or hurting another in any way. Each minor or major action we take, be it unconscious or conscious, whether it through a positive reason or a negative reason.

Love or hate. Whatever we do has a ripple effect on many people's lives. We don't often get to see this effect until we die. This is what is known to be the last judgment. It's not God showing us our wrongs and rights. When we die, we actually see each ripple effect our actions has left in the world. We feel each good deed we did and we also feel each pain we ever created. Our last judgment. We judge ourselves and see for the first time every action created a reaction.

Judgment day isn't about God standing us up against a wall and punishing us for all our sins, instead, it's a process of self-judgment. As spiritual beings, we look back at each action and effect we have left behind. We are able to see the bigger picture on the tidal wave of effects we leave on the physical world. All the pain we may have caused, directly or indirectly we are able to feel. The process of self-judgment is one I believe each and every one of us has to go through at some point in our spiritual existence.

Think of everything you have ever said and done, ever, it would be impossible to imagine how grand the scale where we have reached others is. When we die, we are able to look at it from the outside and see the entire picture. It's an awakening moment. Even those who believe they are good hearted and cause no pain can be surprised how they have left a negative ripple in so many lives.

Of course, judgment day is not only about suffering each pain and bad legacy we have left in the world, but also all the great things that we accomplished and all the joy we have been able to spread around the world. Each time we give and help another, we will be able to feel that joy when our own judgment day comes.

For some of us, we will be happy with our self-judgment, for others it will feel so painful that hell in Heaven is the only description for our reflection.

Fortunately, after we endured our own self-judgment, we are able to choose a way to find a balance in our karma, to be able to help in some way to bring peace and joy to those we have hurt or those who have been affected by us in a negative way.

It is so important to try to minimize any damage or pain whilst living, and if we hurt another person, it is important to try to find our peace whilst we are alive. Death is not an escape, quite the opposite until we balance out our actions, we can still have a lot of work ahead of us on the Other Side.

Home and away

What is now coming to light in the living world is the idea that we can create our own existence to some extent. The same is true of the Spirit world. As Spirits, we can actually create our own existence. Our minds are so powerful, it's similar to a painter with an empty canvas and the ability to paint whatever he chooses, and as Spirit, we can do the same. Once we are back in the Spirit world, we can also create homes. Not a home in the sense we know home. It can't be touched nor dusted, but for the Spirit it's real. I have seen many Spirit homes and I realize Spirit don't always create big mansions to live in, but they do create a place that is surrounded by beauty and holds replicas of artefacts that reminds them of the living world. Much like keeping a souvenir after returning from a holiday.

There are parts of the Spirit world that are almost a replica of the physical world, although I suspect it's actually vice versa, and the little towns with streets and houses where Spirit have set up home has actually been reflected on the earthly world from the Spirit world. It really is quite amazing and more so when you realize it all created with the Spirit mind.

We work and struggle to have a nice home, and yet few of us realize that when we leave this world we can create our very own dream home, literally!

There is an order in the Spirit world much like ours. In fact, the Spirit world seems to have an order about most things. There is a high intelligent order that keeps the Spirit world constantly in balance and constantly evolving. If only that order could also be reflected into our earthly world, we would then have the best of both worlds.

Character

When we die, our character doesn't seem to change very much for quite some time, although we grow and evolve constantly. A shy person will also be a shy Spirit. An overpowering family member will still be overpowering when they have passed. The funny uncle with the huge sense of humour will still be the same once he has passed.

In Spirit, we learn and grow and eventually our character slowly starts to peel away from us in layers. We also learn to disperse of any negative energy. Spirits let go of hate, fear, jealousy, greed and all negative emotion. They live in a world of love and peace, of laughter and joy, and any negative parts of their character are soon forgotten. Partners, who caused great pain to each other in life, often find forgiveness to each other in Spirit. We don't just die and wake up in the Spirit world like this; it's a process we can choose to work on.

Communication

Knowing where Spirits are doesn't help to communicate with them any easier. It only helps to understand the Spirit world more. Because Spirits have no bodies, they communicate with us in many ways.

Direct communication is where Spirit communicates with us without the need of a medium. Thinking of my dad in the morning, hearing his name on the TV just before leaving the house and later hearing his funeral song playing just as I walked into a shop was not a huge coincidence, it was all staged by my dad just to say he was with me. Knowing I needed him around me at that time. Spirit does this constantly and it's important that we realize how much they do this. They communicate directly to us by any means of communication possible.

The page that happened to open whilst looking for something completely different but it took me in an entirely different direction that later help me with a problem I was having, that was Spirit helping and showing me they are with me. That program I didn't realize was on and ended up watching, that lead me to an alighting moment that helped me understand something more about my dad. That wasn't a coincidence. It was his way of showing me what he wanted me to see and understand. The internet, the TV, the radio, these are some electrical goods that Spirit find easy to use or play with, as a means of communicating with us.

Dreams

The other means of easy communication is through our dreams. Most of our dreams are forgotten or are just a part of us venting out feelings and thoughts. Some dreams make no sense and dreams can be a reflection of something that we saw or heard the previous days. However, some dreams are vivid and appear real. They are remembered in a way that we just know it was different. Spirit will communicate with us in dreams. They may actually come directly to us in a dream and show themselves to us, they may pass on a message or they may help us solve a dilemma we are having at the time. Dreams have always been a way Spirit communicate with people and with strong, vivid dreams, we should appreciate them for what they are, Spirit communicating with us. Writing down a dream and taking some time to analyse it is a good way to really appreciate what was shown to us.

I believe I have always used dreams as my easiest way of communication yet not all dreams are easy to understand. Many of my clients tell me about dreams where they have seen their loved ones who have passed over to Spirit. Oddly, many clients dream something scary and most dreams would be better described as nightmares.

For a long time, I couldn't understand why people were dreaming of their loved ones in such a dramatic way, a loved one in pain or crying. Although everyone's dreams were obviously different, the one thing they all have in common is the scary negative feeling my client held onto when waking. I now believe it is all to do with my clients fear or pain of losing their loved one. I believe these "bad" dreams are my client's fear that their loved one is in a bad place or are lost. These dreams are often a reflection of what my client is holding onto regarding the death of their loved one.

Chapter 13

Messages from Spirit

Medium

By using a medium Spirit can often get a direct message across, if you find you are sitting in front of a medium the chances are it's because Spirit has actually sent you there. As more and more people are now learning to become mediums, it has become popular to go to a medium to receive a message from Spirit. As above, so below, and as Spirit teaches us more about communicating with a medium, we advance and produce more mediums each year. Of course, there are still a few people claiming to be mediums who have very little idea, little responsibility, and actually very little Spirit communication, but this happens in all fields of life. There is nothing bigger than people's ego; it's a part of human nature. Using a medium is becoming a popular way for Spirit to bring peace, love or a simple message to a loved one. Just to be able to show they are still around is a joy to Spirit.

Dark night of the soul

Turn right, is something I have heard many people tell apparently lost Spirits, also, light a candle to send them to the light is something that is very common. In all the years, I have communicated with Spirit I have never heard from them about a dark place. Once when I asked Micheal about lighting candles to send people to the light, he laughed at me and asked me if I really believed that God couldn't do something that a simple candle could achieve. There is no dark place where bad people are left to rot. There is no in-between place where Spirits get lost and hang around. There is only a lot of confusion from the living about this subject.

The last judgment that we all make when we encounter the Spirit world is painful enough for those who have been evil or bad in this world. It can be a long, painful inner turmoil for those who have caused pain. The last judgment is not a physical place, it's an inner place.

There is no lost place that I know about. You are in this world living, you die and then you're in the next world. There is no in-between, God creates all his children from the light and we all return to the light. You can't suddenly get lost along the way and be ignored by God and all other Spirit whilst you're left wondering around.

House Spirits or ghosts, as often called, are Spirits that have CHOSEN to hang around a certain place. They may not want to create their own spiritual home and may take a lot longer than some Spirits to realize that the earthly world is a far worse place than the spiritual world. Although a Spirit may choose to stay at a property or a certain place, it doesn't mean they are there constantly, but they choose to still visit the property often or to even live in a physical property but in a spiritual body. It doesn't mean they don't have full spiritual lives, they just choose to keep visiting a certain property. Remember Spirit can be anywhere at any moment just by thought. House Spirits are often seen as negative entities that are stuck in a property. This is not the case. They are just Spirits who for whatever their reason, they prefer to visit a certain property a lot, maybe even live there. It doesn't mean they are not "with the light."

Often, Spirit wants to show people that they are not dead, that they are very much still around. Sometimes they try so hard, their energy can be overpowering and they may scare people whilst trying to prove their existence. Making noises and knocking things over is their way of experimenting with their Spirit energy to see how they can be seen or felt physically. Unfortunately, this scares the hell out of many people and they are immediately classed as a ghost, or worse still, an evil Spirit.

A negative blueprint is one of the scariest real experience a person could have. It can be traumatizing and yet there are no Spirits involved with a negative blueprint. As I briefly explained about psychometry, every single thing in the universe holds energy. Every item, every object, every home, every place holds energies of all things that have happened there. A ring that has been worn by more than one person will hold an essence of the energy of both people who wore it. Energy can never be destroyed, so it will forever hold that energy. By holding that ring we can pick up the energy of one or of both of the people who wore it, depending how tuned in we are.

A children's park that was once a war ground will hold the blueprint of the children playing in wonder and also hold the pain and death of soldiers. Again, it's about how in tune we are when we connect with the energy of the park.

Sometimes energy is captured very much like photo captions, and sometimes like mini films. This is why it's called a blueprint. Any one of us can pick up the image or feeling from a blueprint at any time, and most of us do it on a daily basis at some point.

Going past a certain corner and suddenly feeling cold and shivery, only to find out later that it is the same corner where somebody was murdered. It was probably not the Spirit of the victim you were picking up on. It was the blueprint of what happened there.

Blueprints are confused as actual Spirits so often that people actually believe they are connecting with bad Spirits. It's not, it's just bad memories.

House clearances and all sorts of paranormal cleansing activity are based towards blueprints.

The memory of an incident can be felt by a simple cold feeling or by actually feeling the entire incident. Feeling a blueprint replayed in such a vivid way, if the memory is horrid, it can feel like something from a horror film. The best thing to do if you find yourself getting the horror from a blueprint is to try to ignore it or to leave and stay away from it. If your own home happens to have a negative blueprint, something terrible might have happened in there once and you may feel like that energy still around. The solution is to create as many happy memories in that property as possible. Create so many happy blueprints that you finally live in a happy home that has just a few old negative memories. You will begin to notice more and more the happy blueprints reflecting in the home and only occasionally, the negative ones will come through.

Animals often notice blueprints. Dogs often bark in mid-air at what appears to be nothing. Dogs bark at strange Spirits and they often play with Spirits they know. When animals become Spirits themselves, they go to the same place humans do. They stay in the same parallel world. Animals will stay close to those they have known in life. I've had a lot of readings where Spirit people have shown me they are with their pet. Spirits have passed on messages about being with my clients pets, in much the sense, "don't worry about lassie, he's here with me." Many people receive as much joy connecting with their pets as they do with their family members.

Messages from strangers

Spirit actually use other people to come into our life and express something to us that touch us in one way or another. Often we dismiss these messengers from Spirit as coincidence, but living messengers are a very powerful way of helping and being helped. Have you ever said something to a person and later wondered why you said it, only to find out your words were very helpful? Often we don't realize they were not actually our words. Instead, Spirit was using us in a way to pass on a message.

Have you ever had a complete stranger say something to you that really affected you and became part of your path? Again, this complete stranger was compelled to say those words often-unaware Spirit was working with them.

I remember when I was running a shop and I saw no way out of the economic black hole I was falling deeper into. I found myself desperate. I needed my faith more than ever and it was the time I questioned it the most. It was the one time in my life I felt completely lost and alone, and yet I realized later that it was the time I was the least alone and was helped the most.

Standing behind the counter one day I saw an elderly man walk into the shop, he strolled around and I gave him a pleasant smile. He then approached me, looked me in the eye and said, "You have no twinkle in your eyes, maybe this shop isn't what you are meant to be doing, and maybe it's not part of your life. Sometimes we fight to keep hold of things that are really not meant to be." I was quite taken aback by the stranger's words and really didn't know what to say. Yet I knew that he was right, I was fighting for something that wasn't really meant to be my destiny. He said his words and left. A stranger that I was never to see again. With the work and worry of the shop, I tried to push the stranger's words out of my mind.

Some days later an elderly woman walked into the shop, she began talking to me like she knew me all my life, "It must be hard work running a shop?" she asked, and before I replied she continued, "I bet you have children, don't you, it must be hard trying to bring up children and run a business?" I agreed with her, little did she know just how hard it was, I thought to myself. She then went on to tell me about a business her own daughter had run and the troubles she had encountered. The story was very similar to my own. I wondered why she was really telling me all this. "Sometimes we fight for things that are just not our destiny," she said as she looked into my eyes. "Letting go is hard, but sometimes we have to let go, to get the twinkle back in our eyes," as she said those words I remembered the stranger from a few days earlier. It was an impacting moment for me. The woman smiled at me, explained she was sorry for taking up my time and left.

I decide that day that I had to let go of my shop, no matter what the bank threatened me with. With all the obstacles I was facing I had been determined that I would make my shop a huge success. I was going against all logic and fighting for the shop. That day I realized I didn't want to fight. This wasn't the path to a happy future. I decide to close the business down. To confirm I did the right thing some weeks after closing the shop down somebody commented that my eyes were sparkling, as if I had a twinkle in them.

These two strangers may not even remember their conversation with me. They may have left my shop wondering why they had said those words to me. It doesn't matter, Spirit wanted to talk to me and because I wasn't listening they found another way to get their message across.

I have had encounters similar to this throughout my life, random strangers will talk to me and somehow they will leave me a message, an awakening or a new thought line that will put me back on my right path if I ever I wander.

Spirit are so busy sending us messages and signs by any means possible that it's a shame we don't listen. We should try to take the traffic light code to a spiritual level and stop, look and listen to everything we are seeing and hearing around us before we continue. Certain books will reach us in simple or strange ways, because Spirit wants to give us a message from that book. We encounter people each day in our lives that can help our spiritual growth or help with a current dilemma. We will hear of somebody else's experiences and suddenly realize that it's almost the same as what is happening to us at the time, and we find a different understanding.

Our loved ones in Spirit are communicating with us daily. We just have to learn to see the signs and connect them together, all our solutions, our answers and our learning, is shown to us on a daily basis. Stop, look, and listen are all we have to learn to do.

Part Three

Their Stories

14 Daniel

Forever Friends

The story of Daniel is one that taught me how friendship survives death. It is a story that proved to me that the circle of friendship never dies, instead, that it could even grow in strength after the physical parting. It was early on in my career and I was reading for a woman whom I had never met before, as with most of my readings, I normally don't know the name of the person I am reading for until I check my appointment book, and I rarely have any prior information.

I had only been sitting with my client for a short while, when I felt the Spirit of a teenage lad, he was only 18. At first, the woman could not recognize him until the Spirit showed me the terrible accident of his death. He showed me he had fallen off a roof. I saw the accident quite clearly in my mind as if I was watching a film. When I explained to the woman what I was seeing she recognized him as Daniel, a friend of her daughter, Sheryl.

Daniel seemed very friendly and keen to talk to me. I wasn't sure how the woman felt coming to me for a reading and having contact with her daughter's friend rather than her own relatives. However, Daniel was there loud and clear so I felt I had to pass on any messages he had to say. Daniel was a Spirit I immediately clicked with. He had a sense of humour and I was only young myself at the time so I could understand him in many ways. One of the main messages Daniel wanted to pass on to this woman was that he wanted to talk to her daughter, his friend Sheryl.

It seemed strange passing on that message, why didn't Daniel just say what he wanted to say to the mother. It seemed he wanted to talk to the daughter directly. I asked the woman to pass on a message to her daughter and explain to her that Daniel was trying to communicate with her and maybe she was missing any signs he was sending her, I suggested that Sheryl keeps a dream journal thinking Daniel may try to communicate with her in her sleep.

I liked Daniel, maybe because of his relaxed attitude or maybe it was his insistence to talk to his best friend. I felt good knowing friendships never die.

A few days later, I received a phone call from a young woman who claimed she had to see me for a reading. There was a kind of urgency in her voice. We agreed on a time and the following day she came to see me.

When she arrived at my house, I realized she was only a young girl, maybe a few years older than I was. I could sense she was agitated and although she was a pretty girl, she looked like she was holding the weight of the world on her shoulders. As she sat down at my reading table I noticed the long jumper she was wearing, I thought it was strange as it was a hot summer day. My room was hot so I opened the window; just looking at her in a thick long sleeve jumper on such a sunny day was making me sweat. As I opened the window latch, I felt the presence of Spirit next to me. I sat down in front of the young girl, I recognized the Spirit as Daniel, and in that instant I knew the girl sat in front of me, waiting for me to start the reading was Sheryl. The daughter of the woman I had given a reading for a few days ago.

Daniel immediately wanted to talk to his friend and I passed on many messages that he was telling me. Daniel told me that they had been very close, claiming they were best friends. I could feel how emotional the moment was when Sheryl realized that Daniel was really still with her.

Daniels messages became very serious as he told me how worried he was about Sheryl. This was the reason for her being in my home, although she lived some hours away. When her mum had phoned her up and told her that she had been to a medium and Daniel had come through to her and had wanted to pass a message on to her daughter, Sheryl arranged train times so she could come and see me as soon as she possible. I was soon to find out why

Daniel had insisted he speak to his best friend and why Sheryl felt a long train journey was worth taking.

The moment Daniel showed me the images and told me the message of importance, I blurted it out to Sheryl, "Your boyfriend has been beating you and it's getting worse." I was shocked by my own brutality in my words but I was also feeling the importance of the message from Daniel. His message was loud and clear. "Get out of the relationship now, confide in your mum." It was the last part of his sentence that made me realize why Daniel had not wanted to pass on the message through this girls mum. It was obvious the mother knew nothing about her daughter's abuse.

He had wanted to talk to his friend directly. Then Sheryl burst into tears as she confessed to me that her partner had started beating her shortly after they had moved into their own home together, as they lived some way away, she was able to hide it from her mum. However, the situation was getting worse by the day. It was so bad that she had to cancel her last visit to see her mum because of the amount of bruises she had received in her last beating. She gently rolled her long sleeve up her arm and showed me the bruises she had received. I felt shivers run down my spine as I looked at her purple arm. She didn't know what to do and was too scared to leave her boyfriend. She then went on to recount to me something that had happened a few days previous.

"A few days ago I was sat crying, the fear was affecting every part of me, I never thought I would have become a victim of abuse. I couldn't believe I was in a relationship with such a violent man, yet I still loved him so much. Every inch of my body was hurting me due to the last beating and I was still in pain when he attacked me again. My body was screaming with the pain, yet I was hiding it quite well. He attacked me for silly things, like leaving the milk out or not cooking his dinner the way he liked."

Tears fell like waterfalls down her face as she continued to confide in me, "I was upset and started to think of my closest friend Daniel. I realized how weak I had become since his death and how I still missed him deeply." she took a deep breath and began to weakly smile. "Whilst I was crying, I asked Daniel to help me, I looked up to the sky and I pleaded with him to send me a sign as what I should do. I told him how much I missed him and I knew if he were still alive, he would know what I should do for the best. I felt somehow he was going to help."

She continued recounting her story between tears. "Shortly after I had asked my friend Daniel to help me, I received a phone call from my mum. She sounded quite excited as she told me about her visit with you and how Daniel had come through and he had been trying to contact me." Sheryl said she took her mum's phone call as the sign she had asked for and needed. Sheryl planned her train journey without telling her boyfriend. She knew it was a big risk for her because her boyfriend would go ballistic when he found out. Yet at the same time, she had an uncontrolled desire to come and see me.

I felt like an outsider as I passed on messages from Daniel to his friend, their friendship was so strong. It was stronger than death. Daniel still loved and cared for his friend just as he would if he had been alive. "Daniel is the only person I would have told about my abuse," she told me. I witness the love between the two friends first hand and I suddenly felt a part of them both.

Sheryl left my house knowing that Daniel was still with her, he still cared for her that the love was just as strong as when he was alive. Daniel showed me how the love of a friend is just as strong as the love of a family member.

Sheryl did not return to her boyfriend, but instead went to her mum's house and told her mum all about her ordeal since leaving the family home. She moved back in with her mum who slowly healed her from her physical and emotional trauma. She realized she loved herself more than she loved her partner. Sheryl also realized her partner needed help and she was not the one who was able to give him the help he needed. He had his own journey ahead of him. He needed to want to change.

However, for me, the story of Daniel did not stop there. I was in my kitchen one day and I hadn't even realized I had been talking to Daniel until he made me laugh and I found myself laughing aloud. I began my own friendship with him. I felt his presence on a regular basis and for the next few months, I had readings for many people who knew him. I would be in the middle of a reading and he would appear. It seemed he was sending me his family and friends to pass on messages, enabling them to understand that not only was he happy and at peace with his death, but he still had the same sense of humour and the same character he did when he was alive. Death changes very little in a person.

Not only did Daniel show me the strength of friendships after death, but he also showed me how we are able to make friendships even after death. I consider Daniel to be a friend. Although our first meeting was many years ago and I have not had him turn up in a reading for years, even now I still have visits from him every now and then.

Daniel was only young; he had what others would say his whole life ahead of him. He was a good young man who worked hard and kept himself and those around him happy. He brought no trouble to his family and was a happy soul. In Spirit he came through with that same happiness and that same caring side to him he had in life. He accepted his death as part of life itself and he came through with many details of his life that only those who knew him could confirm. He came to show his friends that he was still the same Daniel as ever, he still cared for them he still watched out for them.

It is an exciting feeling knowing that friendships never die and can be built upon or even created in the afterlife. There is an old saying, we cannot choose our families, but we can choose our friends. I believe we choose both family and friends before we start our journey of life. For whatever reason we have chosen the family we were born with, whether we like them or not, they are all part of our life destiny.

Over the years, I have given readings where there have been broken friendships involved. I once had a woman for a reading whose friend came through in Spirit, the Spirit friend wanted to tell my client that she was happy and well on the Other Side and that she was sorry they had fallen out.

"But does she accept she was wrong?" my client quizzed me.

The Spirit woman said she did not feel she was wrong at the time of what I was now working out had been a huge row between them both. The Spirit woman was showing me there was no wrong or right, it was something that had happened between them both. Yet she wanted my client to know how much she always loved her, and how sorry she was they had lost so much time in their friendship.

"No no no," said my client waving a finger at me. "If she's not going to admit she was wrong, then I don't want to know or hear anything about her again." My client started raising her voice as she continued, "I don't want to see her again, I don't want her to come near me anymore, and I don't want any contact from her at all."

I took a deep breath and calmly said to her, "She's dead, your friend has come from the Afterlife, to give you a message saying she was sorry you had both fallen out, we are talking dead – Afterlife."

"Well, she better stay dead for a very long time," my client replied. I gathered this friendship was well and truly over. It's not the first time I have had a client refuse to make amends with a friend who has passed. I often wondered why you wouldn't forgive Spirit. Until some years ago, another client came to me for a reading. She also received a message from her ex-best friend asking for forgiveness of how the situation had turned sour between them. My client refused point blank to speak to her. I asked my client why she wouldn't forgive her friend.

She thought about it for a while and then calmly told me that she understood her friend was in a place of peace and joy, her friend had time to review her life and to see the errors and the certain roads that had been taken, but she, my client wasn't in that place. She wasn't in a place of peace and joy, she didn't have time to review her life and she couldn't stand back from her life and see the reasons certain things happened. I thought it was a pretty fair argument. Not everyone is ready to forgive the moment Spirit come and speak. I can only hope that Spirit communication can open a door for freeing the past at some point.

15 Judy

A Mothers Mistakes

I had a reading for a woman whose name was Liz who brought a friend with her for the reading, her friend's name was Julia and she promised to sit in silence. I always ask if a person really wants their friend to sit in on a reading, and a majority of them do, although I do not recommend it. The experience of Liz taught me that Spirit will use whatever means they can to communicate.

Almost immediately, I felt a Spirit presence. However, it wasn't for Liz, instead, for her friend Julia, who I could feel was embarrassed for taking up her friends reading time, but at the same time intrigued to receive a message for herself. I felt the energy from the mother of Julia come through to me in Spirit. The mothers name was Judy and she expressed how very sorry she was for the way she had treated Julia throughout her life, she said she had desperately tried to make her peace with her daughter since her passing. Julia's emotions were very high as her mother told me about her own alcohol problem she had endured for years. Judy blamed her alcohol addiction for being the reason that had prevented her from being the mum she had wanted to be. She then told me that Julia had followed in her footsteps and had suffered her own alcohol problems.

The mother was desperately trying to apologize to her daughter for not being around whilst she was alive. Yet she was showing me how much she had been around since her death. Judy showed me experiences of her daughter's life that she had been part of since her passing.

Julia had a lifetime of emotions hit her all at once, the loneliness she had felt from her mother and the abandonment she felt throughout her childhood. However, I could feel the love between them. It seemed like a longer than normal reading for me as I passed on messages of forgiveness and regrets between daughter and mother. Nicole was only a small child at the time and I remember Julia's experience reminded me never to let regret come between me and my daughter. I felt the pain between both the daughter and the Spirit of the mother and I promised myself that no matter what, if I died tomorrow, I would not want to return with messages of regret and forgiveness.

Julia didn't forgive her mother immediately, but the conversations they had helped them both on the road to peace. Julia was able for the first time to see it from a lost, drunken mother's point of view, and find an understanding with her past. Knowing that her mother was in Spirit trying to be as close as she wasn't in life made Julia feel more compassion and closeness with her mother than ever.

Julia was in her early 50s and her mum had passed several years earlier. There had been such a distance between them ever since Julia could remember and Judy had confessed during the reading that it was mostly down to Judy's own drinking problem that finally took her life. Julia was left with nothing more than bad memories and a heap of resentment. She never expected her mum to come to her and ask for forgiveness.

This was the first time I had ever encountered the reading to be for the friend who just came along rather than the person who came for the reading. I felt slightly out of control, but I knew I had to continue. Something told me within that I had to follow my intuition. There is always a reason for everything.

At first, Liz, who the reading was actually for, had seemed happy that her friend was receiving messages from her mother, but as the messages became deeper and the conversation more intense I could feel her wanting for it to end and for Spirit to communicate with her. This was very early on in my career and I wasn't sure how to handle this situation, but I knew, even then, that Spirit had to come first. I couldn't ask this Spirit mother who had waited so long to make the peace to move over, as somebody else wanted my time.

The entire session between Julia and Judy took quite a while. Tears, emotions, and laughter were shared, and I feel Julia really received years of answers in that session. Unfortunately, after the communication, I was too exhausted to feel anything else. Liz didn't get a reading that day from me, just a lot of apologies. I hoped she was the friend she claimed to be and was happy that her closest friend was able to start the journey of peace with her mother.

Judy had seen an opportunity to jump in and make her peace, to express her forgiveness. She had been trying in dreams to communicate with her daughter, but Julia hadn't wanted to think of her mum. Therefore, she placed any signs or communication she was receiving to the back of her mind. Often she remembered dreams of confusion and negative, dark feelings, I feel that was Julia's own feelings about her mother. It was only when the perfect situation came about that her mum was able to communicate with her clearly.

Only after the reading and after my apologies to Liz for her disappointment in not receiving any messages for herself, is when I found out that it was Julia who had originally been given my number from a friend. Julia didn't really believe in the Spirit world, but she knew her friend Liz did believe and actually, it was Julia who phoned me for the appointment. Liz had no phone at the time.

When Liz was due to come to me for a reading she began to feel nervous and decided she couldn't do it alone. Therefore, she asked her friend Julia to come along. I assume Liz wanted her friend to come and sit in silence and witness whatever was to come about in the reading. Julia reluctantly agreed to come along and sit in on the session. Not knowing how this was about to change her life on some level.

I spoke to Julia some time later when she brought other clients to me. She looked different and she told me that she completely believed in the Spirit world now. Not only did she believe, but also she confessed she was starting to communicate with Spirit herself. More importantly, she also told me she had been able to forgive her mother and instead of holding on to feelings of loneliness and hate, she now realized it was her mother who had been lonely in life. She also understood for the first time that her mother had an illness that wasn't treated or accepted. Instead, it was hidden from the world, other than from those who were closest to her, like Julia.

I think what touched me the most about this story of mother and daughter was that Julia admitted that for the first time she understood that her mother's behaviour had been nothing personal. Her mother had treated her badly, and she was now very sorry for that treatment. It doesn't mean Julia suddenly forgets what happened to her, but now she can accept it for what it was, nothing personal and something that is now in her past. Julia told me that knowing her mother was suffering for her actions, knowing she took responsibility and was asking for forgiveness, even after death, gave Julia a way of setting her past free.

I felt the pain Judy had lived whilst alive and the pain she still lived since her passing. Both different pains, but both due to her lack of being the mum she had always wanted to be. She had let life take her over and only in death was she able to make the peace. Her mission for peace was so strong that she bombarded another person's reading to get her message across.

After the reading with Liz, I tried to avoid people turning up with friends, but since then and thousands of readings later I realize that sometimes it's a way for Spirit to connect. I feel there is a bigger plan at work, if we direct A to the reading with B then that's the only way we can get our message to B loud and clear.

Of course, this situation doesn't always happen. I have often had people turn up for a reading with a friend. The friend hasn't been mentioned or hardly noticed by me in the reading, but every now and then the reading becomes about the friend. As long as I explain what could happen before the reading and I feel everyone is happy with the possible outcome I then let fate take its turn.

If you do decide to go to a medium and you choose to take a friend with you, just keep in mind that sometimes the reading could be turned around and become about your friend, you could be ignored for the entire reading, don't despair. Remember this is what friends are for. The reading had probably been pre-planned by Spirit. See it for the magic that it is. Be happy for your friend and for the Spirit person. One way or another, your time will come for you to communicate with your loved ones.

More importantly, Judy's message is a reminder for us not to regret our actions in life. No matter what, there is still time to change, still time to make peace with those we love, it doesn't matter how hard the task may feel, how much damage is done, now is the moment to start to make peace with all those we love. If we die without that peace, then have to work harder on the Other Side to bring our simple message across, whilst alive, we have letters, email, phones, we also have travel, a train ride a car ride or for some people it's just a walk away to reunite with a loved one and make peace.

On the Other Side, it is a lot harder, as Judy showed me she had been trying to jump into her daughters dreams, she had spent years trying to ask for forgiveness and understanding, only to have her efforts fall on deaf ears, ears that couldn't hear her.

It's never too late to be the mother, father, friend or spouse that we really wanted to be. Don't wait for death to start the journey.

16 Antony

A Single Yellow Rose

It really is the smallest details that can make the entire difference from a person not believing to believing they have connected with their loved ones who passed. Why does Spirit not come and give their names and addresses, their shoe size and their date of birth? It is one of the most asked questions I am asked. The answer is very simple. Why should they? Surely, people know who their own relatives or loved ones are. When my mum phones me up, she does not start the conversation with her name and address, her date of birth and her shoe size. This is something she most surely has not thought about before contacting me. She knows I will recognize her as my mum. She will then go on to talk about bits and pieces of interesting chitchat and somewhere in the conversation she will tell me if she is well or not, she will give me advice on something she may feel she wants to then she will say her goodbyes and hang up. If I do ask when answering the phone, "Who is it?" I will get the helpful reply of, "It's me."

Spirits are very much the same. There is a process going on and Spirit often don't think about the simple sending of the facts, yet they do send important information to us and from that we gather a communication that is worth much more than their date of birth, as in the story of Antony.

A woman named Ann came to see me for a reading. I felt the Spirit energy of her son Antony, who had passed a few years previous. He was a young man, early twenties, and he immediately showed me the love him and his mum shared. Antony showed me little bits of information about his life, his memories, and his feelings. I received symbols in my mind that was quite clear to understand.

I had not yet been told by Antony how he had died until I suddenly saw pizzas in my mind, yes, I was seeing many pizzas. At first, I was confused with the image I was seeing so I told Ann exactly what I was seeing. "Your son is strangely showing me lots of pizzas," his mum nodded and said she could understand that. I figured he may have worked in a pizza place and continued with the other images I was seeing. However, later on, the pizzas came back to me. This time, there were lots of them. I could see pizzas and then food everywhere. Suddenly my body felt sick and I felt five times bigger than I was. I then understood what I was seeing and feeling.

"Your son died of obesity," I said. Antony's mum confirmed that was how he died so young. He ate himself to death.

There was no doubt in my mind Antony had tried his best to show his mum, not only that he was at peace and happy, but that he was with her often. He also showed his loving, caring, personality, just as his mum knew him. He shared his constant love for her and recognized the pain she was still suffering due to his death. He shared silly details of his past, like programs they would watch together, places they had visited together, that to a stranger or a sceptic who wants facts and figures make no sense. However, to a mother hearing the real memories and thoughts of her son, no matter how small and silly was more than proof that Antony was communicating with her.

I felt true sadness inside me whilst connecting this mother and son. The pain and the hurt I was feeling from the mother and at the same time, the love I was feeling from Antony for Ann was overwhelming.

I have never cried in front of a client, yet when Ann left I spent days crying. The beauty of the reading was Ann realizing her son was still with her, it was a truly comforting moment for her. Yet still I could feel her grief strongly. I am human and Antony, with all his words of love, all his happy memories, all his proof he was still mummy's boy, it broke my heart. He talked about his despair with his illness that eventually killed him. I understood obesity in a completely different way. The suffering Antony had endured because of his weight and to eventually die due to it was something I had never understood previously.

The way the world judged him and looked at him. The way he was ridiculed and bullied by others, left out of society because he was too big. His only comfort was the love from his mother and food. He would find comfort in the very thing that was hurting him. Yet he focused more on the fun parts of his life, how close he was to his mother, the happier memories. Although he was a lonely boy, with no friends, he was still able to recall some happy memories.

It was the very last detail where I learned how little details are the most important to people. Just as I felt my communication with Antony was ending, I saw one single yellow rose. Antony had shown his mum so much proof he was still with her I really didn't need to say anymore. Yet he showed it to me again. As just as the last word I casually said, "Oh, one very last thing, Antony is showing me one single yellow rose," on hearing my words Ann jumped up and down with tears of joy and bounced around my room.

I sat in surprise at first and waited for her to calm down and explain the hysteria. She proceeded to tell me that when her son had died she had placed a single yellow rose in his coffin; it had been their special flower. She also said that she had asked Antony that if he was to ever contact her to show her the yellow rose. Although she had been happy with the reading so far, it was that minor small detail at the end that proved to her that her son was really with her and was communicating with her. He had not forgotten the yellow rose.

I was not really going to even mention it, it came at the end of the reading and I was about to close it down. In any split second, I could have easily been happy with the reading so far and ignored that little minor detail.

However, I have in the past ignored minor details, although I now try my hardest not to, but the entire process is like a huge puzzle and sometimes we try to put one piece in before another. So many people go to mediums with such huge expectations. If you did not get what you really wanted maybe, you got what you needed. Maybe the medium did not pick up the important detail you wanted, but picked up on other information that you could connect with also. Having high expectations when you go to see a medium is the quickest way to disappointment.

I have had people come to me and they have received very good Spirit communications with their loved ones. Nevertheless, they have still left disappointed because the one magic word, the one secret, the one detail that connects them in their heart completely did not get a mention. Often that one thing is not the name and addresses. It is a personal connection.

Do not be disappointed if you do not get the message that you want, the one you had expected. Antony's mum had been to several mediums before she had been to me. I was the only one who picked up on him and his messages and the only one who noticed his yellow rose. That does not mean to say I am any better than the others are. It just means I connected more on that day.

Antony's story really opened my eyes to the smaller details of Spirit communication. Up until then I had also been asking Spirit why they don't come through with secret codes and bank account numbers, home telephone numbers and their street name. However, I realized this is cold information that is just facts and figures. The intimate details are the ones that reach people. Since then I can honestly say that I have witnessed repeatedly how people get pleasure out of the smaller things in life and death.

Antony wanted his mum to actually feel like he was there with her, to show her he hadn't changed. He wanted to remind her of the love they both shared, the life they both lived together. He wanted to come, chat, and show his love to his mum. That's what he did. Ann knew that day when she left my house that she had just sat and had a conversation with her son. She knew that he had made her laugh and cry. She knew without a doubt that he was still with her. Only the minor details can allow this to happen. Antony will hold a very special place in my heart and it is thanks to the importance of the yellow rose I understand the importance of each detail of my readings no matter how minor they may appear.

Antony has been important in my path at realizing how very comforting and important my work as a medium can be. The compassion I have for each reading I give, for each Spirit I encounter and for each message I pass on between worlds, Antony and his caring, loving Spirit has left that impact on me finding my own inner compassion in my work as a medium.

17 Marc

A True Hero

Early on in my career as a medium, I was invited to participate in a psychic fair. It seemed like a huge event for me at the time and I was tremendously eager and excited. On arriving at the large building where the event was to take place I became very nauseous. Many people were to enter the big double doors that night. I noticed there were quite a lot of other readers, part of me wished with so many readers, I would just disappear into the background and not be noticed yet, there was a stronger version of me inside of myself telling me that I could do this, I could give readings to strangers in a public place. I wanted to be a working medium; this was a chance for me.

I arranged my table in a way it looked almost like everyone else's, crystals, Angels, Tarot cards and incense placed out neatly on my pretty purple tablecloth and I felt comfortable.

The night was a huge success for me for many reasons. Firstly, because I was able to do nine readings, for me at the time it was the most I had ever done in one evening and it seemed like nine hundred. I realized I was capable of hiding my own lack of confidence and I surprised myself as to how professional I was. It was very early in my career and I was so young yet it was my warm up to the work I wanted to do.

However, my true success of the night was the story of Marc.

A young girl who looked about my age sat in front of me for a reading, she had pale skin and blonde hair. She was dressed very modern and as I noticed how pretty she looked, that's also when I realized my grey outfit and my ugly shoes were a huge mistake. I realized I didn't look sophisticated or mature, I just looked odd, like a young girl in a huge suit.

I was second-guessing about the wonderful life she probably had. She was so pretty, I bet she had a boyfriend and spent hours on the phone with him, whilst I spent hours talking to the dead, I imagined she would take time painting her nails and styling her hair, whilst I spent the same time meditating and jumping between worlds.

My thoughts were interrupted as I saw lots of water in my mind. I saw water, then I felt a feeling of drowning. As I felt myself drowning I saw an image of my own dad, all this happened within seconds in my mind's eye, but I was able to put it all together and blurt out to the young girl, "Your father died by drowning."

Her eyes opened and I actually saw the hairs on her arms stand up, "Yes he did," she replied. I could feel the Spirit energy of a man by her side; I could feel him very strongly. He came through showing me how much love he had for his daughter. His name was Marc.

Marc had drowned whilst out one day with his friend. He swam out to sea to save his friend's life who was drowning yet had ended up drowning himself. He was a true hero. He was only young and he seemed like a caring, loving father. He had been a low-income dad and he loved spending time with his daughter. It was no surprise to me that he wanted to tell his daughter he was still with her, still watching her, a message that is so often repeated by Spirit. Marc also commented on things he had witnessed since his death, like his daughter's new haircut and her new job. He commented on her new boyfriend and spoke about other members of the family, including his girlfriend he had been seeing at the time of his death and how he had also been by her side. Marc wanted to show his daughter that although his physical presence was gone he was still very much around and was still participating in the family.

The young girl seemed dazzled by the messages of love from her father, for one moment I stopped and realized how much I missed my own dad, my entire life.

Marc kept returning to his heroic moment that lead to his death, at first, I assumed it was because he had been a true hero, but then I realized that wasn't the message he was repeating to me, he was lingering on his death more than most Spirits do because it was an issue I had to address. He showed me his daughter was full of anger and resentment. In a way she felt like her father had chosen his friend's life over his own, not considering the effects it would have on her life. She felt bitter and disappointed at her father for leaving her.

Marc was showing me he didn't want his daughter to see his death as something he had chosen over her, but instead as part of his character of being a very sensitive, honest, caring, and loving person. Marc was attempting to teach his daughter to let go of his death. "Let go of any situation that you can't control in life." Marc wanted to tell his daughter. He wanted her to let go of anger and disappointment and realize that time can never be turned back, what to us seems like a cruel hand of fate is actually part of a perfectly set plan of destiny. His daughter was going to have to live with the loss of her dad for her entire life and Marc wanted to make sure she remembered him with laughter and joy, not with tears of resentment.

Saying to a young girl that her dad is dead because "that's destiny," is a harsh message to give. Yet Marc was explaining it to his daughter through me in a way that even I was understanding, she had to let go of his death and hold on to the joy of his life, and above all, she had to get on with her own life knowing her dad will always be by her side.

Marc explained to me that life is mapped out perfectly, there are no accidents nor are there any unplanned deaths, he wrote his death before he was born. For whatever reason, reasons that may never become apparent in our lifetime, most things are the way they are destined to be. No matter how painful and even cruel it may seem, we have to learn to let go of the want to change and our need to find sense. The hardest lesson we will ever learn in life is to let go.

My client had to rejoice in her dad's life and understand him. Marc didn't swim out to sea to die, nor to leave his daughter, he swam out to sea because he would never have been able to live with himself if he had just sat and watched his friend die in front of him. To do nothing in such a situation was not who Marc was, and his daughter had to learn to understand him and his decisions. He wanted her to let go of the tears of resentment and instead to hold onto the tears of joy and the celebration of his life.

It was a powerful reading between father and daughter, her makeup was now streaming down her face as she had cried throughout the reading. I had spent a lot longer with the reading than I was advised to, yet I felt a change in energy with this young girl. I really felt as if her father had been able to get the message across to her and somehow heal her anger. I was excited with myself as I realized I was doing the work I had always wanted to do. Yet it was the very last part of the reading that surprised me. Marc actually thanked me.

This was the first time I had ever been verbally thanked by Spirit and it brought home to me how the readings are not only for myself, nor for the client, but how important they are for Spirit. It is what gives me strength to constantly try to become a better medium.

18 Jack

Medium in the Middle

Paula came to me in the hope of reaching her dad Jack. I hadn't known that was her reason at the time. Spirit are not dial on command so I always advise people not to come with expectations of who may connect with me from the Spirit world. People may come wanting desperately to have contact from one loved one who has passed and may receive contact from several others but not the one they had hoped for. There are many reasons for this, one reason being it could be the fault of the medium. Sometimes I can feel a lot of Spirit energy around a person whilst doing a reading. However, I reach out and connect with the one I feel closest to me. The one I feel I can connect to most clearly. Other times I don't have much choice, out of several Spirit I feel around me one will be louder or chattier than the others. Therefore, I have little choice but to listen and pass on messages.

A medium cannot say, sorry you are not important enough in this person's life, go away because they want contact from someone else. There are also other reasons for this. Maybe a Spirit has been contacting their living loved ones in other ways. In dreams, through signs, music, or directly to them. Therefore, they may feel there is no real need in that moment to come and communicate. Alternatively, as funny as it may sound, they may just not have much to say.

However, Paula did get contact from her dad. It was lovely contact that reminded me again just how much some daughters and fathers are so close. Jack seemed like a caring dad who showed this side of his character when he came through in the reading. He gave out memories and details that Paula knew without a doubt that it was her dad who was communicating. He then went on to send his love to his other daughter. Not wanting to forget about her.

The reading was very emotional for Paula, but she got great joy and peace knowing her dad was still involved with her life. Knowing he was still with her and around her, sharing in her life since he had passed. He mentioned things in her life that had happened since he had passed and she got a great sense of happiness knowing he had been around. Paula described to me the peace she felt knowing her dad was still with her.

The next day I had a reading for another woman. The reading was good. There was quite a lot of Spirit contact. Family relatives and a close friend all came with messages for her and all showed themselves to me very clearly. There was a lot of love around this woman. However, after the reading finished she suddenly burst into tears. When I asked her what was wrong, she told me that Paula was her sister and yesterday after the reading I gave, Paula had gone to her sisters and told her almost word for word what had happened in the reading. Explaining in detail their dad's communication from Spirit.

Now this woman was in tears asking why her dad hadn't wanted to speak to her, why had he only come through for his sister?

I explained to her the best way I could. There could be many possible reasons for this. Maybe Jack had used a lot of energy the day before to communicate so he was quieter today, therefore, I never noticed him. Maybe yesterday his messages were for them both. He probably knew that Paula was going to immediately go to her sisters and share the reading word for word. Maybe today he wasn't around. Spirits, although dead have very much a busy life. Maybe he just wasn't able to return to me to today to give a message to his other daughter. I was sure of one thing. I was sure that Jack loved both his daughters and I was sure he was using far more ways than a medium to communicate with them both.

On further inquiry, his daughter did tell me that she has a lot of her own contact with her dad, she dreams of him often. She feels him around her often. Whenever she is reaching an important decision in her life, she can actually smell him and she can feel him helping her to the best way forward.

Actually, it seemed that Jack had been making a lot of contact with his daughter and she had felt it often over the years. She was able to see that she didn't need a medium to contact her father. He had never really left her. She was then able to look at the other messages she had received from other Spirits that day. Moreover, accept them for what they were; messages of love from her Spirit loved ones.

The story of Jack bothered me for a while after. I wondered how many people actually left a reading after having Spirit contact, but left disappointed because it wasn't whom they had wanted to communicate with. This is why I constantly repeat my message of no expectations. I really hope people don't miss the magic that Spirit can send us in their messages because it wasn't the Spirit they wanted to hear from.

We tend to put people in lines of importance, children, parents, siblings, grandparents, and so forth, ending with people, we know and who may have slightly affected us in life, like schoolteachers or neighbours. However, Spirit doesn't put us in lines of importance. Your old schoolteacher could have just as much an important message for you as your Grandfather. We each affect a person's life in one way or another. We send out a domino of effects that ripple throughout life and death.

To be disappointed because you didn't get the Spirit come through that you wanted may be a natural reaction. However, if you do go to a medium and someone else you know comes through, please accept it for the joy it is intended to bring. It takes Spirit a lot of energy to be able to connect with a medium. Don't spoil it by being fussy.

I thank Jack for coming to me during Paula's reading and due to the lack of communicating with him the following day I was able to learn a big lesson from Spirit that has walked with me every step of my work as a medium. I have no control whatsoever about who will communicate with me, what they may show me or what message they may pass on. I really am just the medium in the middle.

19 David

The Sunflower

I had a large friendly lady arrive at my home for a reading. All I knew about her was her name was Jackeline. Her father David came to me in Spirit. David showed me many personal memories with his daughter. He showed me details that proved to Jackeline that it was her father talking to her. He also showed me things that were very personal to them both. It was a lovely reading. David being a very calm and peaceful energy expressed his love for Jackeline and told me he would always walk with her when she needed him.

He showed me his battle with cancer had been very hard on his family and he was no longer in pain. Also, other details, including his mother's Spirit had come to him whilst he was passing and had helped him pass to the Spirit world.

There were two details that he showed me and for some reason I always remembered. He showed me that whilst he had suffered from cancer he had been very well treated by the staff at the hospice he had stayed in, he really wanted to pass that message on. "The staff there are fantastic, they really helped," he told me.

He explained how well he had been treated and how he was glad of his family's decision to place him in the hospice. David then showed me a huge sunflower, in my mind all I could see was this really big sunflower. I passed the information to Jackeline. She was obviously very happy to hear from her dad, she told me the sunflower was the name of the ward he was staying at in the hospice, the sunflower ward.

David showed me that the sunflower was also present at his funeral and he liked it very much.

Jackeline told me her dad was so happy and well looked after at the hospice for the last journey of his life that at the funeral everyone wore little sunflower pins.

David went on to talk about his funeral in detail, what music was played, who attended and who didn't. It seemed he felt he had a good send off and it was clear he had been present throughout the day.

I thought the entire session was really beautiful. It wasn't until after the reading that Jackeline told me her father had died that very same week.

I have since had countless Spirits talk about their own funerals, as Spirits seem to like to attend.

There is another reason I remember David and his sunflower but I wasn't to find out until some 13 years later when my own stepdad, Rick, took ill due to cancer. A devastating time for the family as anyone who has had cancer eat away at a loved one will understand. Rick had wanted to move back to a place he had lived for many years, and after the biggest nightmare any wife could imagine, my mother took her sick husband back to where he wanted to die. My mother had nursed him each and every step of the way but when she arrived back in the town they had both once lived, unfortunately, she had to move again almost immediately to another accommodation.

Those few days were so hard for her. Moving from one place to a next then a few days later moving again to the town next door. My stepsister Leah, a real daddy's girl, left her home with her children, Holly and Spencer and also moved town to be closer to her dad. I flew over from Spain back to England and my stepbrother came from the army to help with the move. We were all there to help, but moving with a sick man is an almost impossible task, and against everything my mum had wanted, as he was deteriorating so quickly and he also needed more tests done on him, we were forced to put him in a hospice for a few days whilst we all helped with the house move.

I hadn't been back in this town for years myself. It was the same town I had been living during the time I had given the reading for

Jackeline. We all arrived at the hospice. As I walked in through the doors, I suddenly felt a familiar energy. I do not know how I distinguish one energy from another, but suddenly I thought of David. Then I saw it, there on the wall was a huge sunflower. It was the same sunflower ward in the same hospice where David had stayed. His words, although 13 years old, came flooding back to me. "The staff there are fantastic, they really helped," I felt a huge wave of relief come over me. I knew Rick was going to be looked after. I had no doubt, and he was. The few days he was in there the staff were fantastic. It gave us all time to be able to house move so he could come home to a comfortable place to die. How one Spirit man gave me peace some 13 years after his passing is still part of life's magic to me. I hold a special place in my heart for David.

20 *Tanya*

Angel Wings

I had a Reading for a lady named Ana, a lovely, tall, attractive lady with long brown hair, no fancy frills or makeup yet there was a lovely radiance of peace and beauty with her. Almost as soon as Ana sat down for the reading I felt a very strong presence of a Spirit. I could feel myself becoming hot and for a moment, I felt like nothing around me was real. The Spirit showed herself to me as a young girl. Ana confirmed she had a daughter, Tanya, who passed in her teens. If there ever was a Spirit that I have encountered that was full of life, full of fun and talked and talked it was Tanya. She came across just as she had been in life. She was happy and I could actually feel her happiness filling up inside me as if her happiness was contagious in some way.

Tanya showed me many personal details, minor things that her mom recognized immediately; she also showed me details of her life and her passing. Tanya had died from heart problems, she had problems for some time and Tanya knew she was going to die. From what she was showing me, her illness had never stopped her from living, even at such a young age, she had lived a very full and active life, not being scared of anything including death.

One of the first things I was seeing during the reading was wings. I could see wings, I tried to think what that meant and my first thought was of Angels, she was showing me something to do with Angels, but then I saw a drawing, a black ink drawing of wings, two Angel wings. As I told Ana what I was seeing I realized what my mind was seeing, just then Ana told me what I was seeing was a tattoo of Angel wings that Tanya had done. Although a small piece of information, for her mother it was very significant. Tanya had really wanted the Angel wings tattoo and had been able to accomplish her wish before she passed.

I could have spent hours with Tanya, as every piece of information she was showing me was important and significant to her mum. Tanya also went on to show me the love she had for her brother and her stepdad, whom to her was someone she loved dearly. Having the same blood doesn't make a dad, but caring and loving a child, being there for her, listening and laughing, all these things are what makes a dad. How could a young teenager be so much wiser than most adults were?

Tanya showed me things that had changed since her passing, things her brother had been doing and family occasions that had all happened since she passed, again Ana confirmed all the information. It was Tanya's way of proving she hadn't left the family, that whenever she wanted, whenever the need she could always "pop" home and spend time with the family.

However, Ana already knew this. Ana was different from most people that came to me for a reading in the hope of receiving Spirit contact because Ana had her own contact with her daughter. Ana knew without a doubt that her daughter was still around and was happy in the next world. Ana had felt Tanya's presence since her passing, all the information I was giving to Ana was lovely confirmation. Ana explained to me not only did she feel her daughter's presence, but she also had dreams that confirmed her feelings. Ana was definitely more advanced with the understanding of Spirit and the Spirit world than most people who came for readings were.

Because of this, because I knew Ana didn't want to see me for help with her own grief, because I knew she didn't need me and would not become dependent on me, I agreed when some time later she asked to come to see me again. Over the years, I built up a friendship with Ana, Tanya, and Tanya's stepdad, whom by the way is the only Spanish man I know who looks like a Scottish lord. Normally I don't like to repeat readings for people who are still grieving and although the Spirit of a loved one comes through very strong it doesn't mean they will come again. Ana knew this and never expected Tanya to come, in fact, she would have been happy to have an old friend turn up, like I said Ana is very spiritually connected.

Tanya did connect with me again on quite a few occasions. Once she showed me a picture of herself with a friend. In the picture, Tanya was wearing a bandana around her head, Ana confirmed the existence of this picture. That was the first time I actually saw what she looked like, although not the last, as some time later I saw Tanya walking with a child, this child had been brought up before by Tanya, but it was a piece of information neither I nor Ana understood.

Tanya unusually showed me information about her parent's future, she told me she wanted her mum to get married. I was slightly shocked at repeating this as I was sure Ana and her partner were married, but Ana confirmed they were not married.

Tanya then showed me an image of her mother pregnant, she showed me a baby in a cot with a mobile hanging above, a lovely chubby baby. I told Ana and her partner what I was seeing. To my surprise, they were very happy with this news, they had both wanted another baby, but Ana was worried she was becoming "too old." Well, Tanya obviously has inside information.

I was over the moon some time later when I found out Ana and her lookalike Scottish lord were pregnant. I was amazed with Tanya's ability's and I remembered Tanya's excitement about her mother's pregnancy. Sometime later Ana had a dream, black liquid was dripping from her womb and dripping between her legs, we both knew when she told me about the dream what it meant. Shortly after her dream, it was confirmed that Ana had a miscarriage.

At first, I was very upset, not only for Tanya's parent's loss, but I also felt guilty, I wondered why Tanya had showed me in great detail a baby in a cot, why show me the mobile hanging above the cot with a chubby baby lying inside if it wasn't going to be. I felt guilty I had passed on the news of false hope, yet I also knew that Spirit doesn't normally make predations as they are not our fortune tellers. The few times they have shown me news of something to come, it has always been for a reason. I felt Tanya had wanted her mum to have the news of the birth to show Ana she wasn't too old and it was going to happen, and not only did she have Tanya's blessing to have another child but that Tanya was ecstatic about it. Now nothing made sense.

It was quite some time later when Ana and her partner came to see me. I was very happy to see them, she told me all about her wedding, how wonderful it had been, and how she had known Tanya was with her on the day. They also introduced me to their newborn baby boy, a beautiful chubby baby with a beautiful smile, after the miscarriage Ana had got pregnant again. This time, Tanya's new brother was born. I almost cried when I held him. I wondered if his soul could still remember how much he was wanted and what wonderful parents he has. I wondered how many times in his lifetime, he would also feel Tanya's presence.

Tanya taught me so much about trust, it really is hard to just sit back and trust, even after meeting the Spirit of Tanya, after all the correct information she had given me, I still doubted her when Ana had her miscarriage, I never thought maybe Ana would become pregnant again. It just never occurred to me. I should have just trusted Tanya.

In my readings with Tanya three other pieces of information came about, she had told me her mum had been writing something short about her, Ana confirmed that she had made a photo album of Tanya and her wonderful short but happy life, under each photo Ana had placed a little saying. Tanya also showed me a picture of a rainbow, I could see this picture in my head clearly, yet Ana could not recognize a picture of a rainbow. Later that evening whilst I was in my bedroom, I was sat thinking about Tanya and her amazing communication, as I looked up I saw a picture lying up against my wall, my daughter had drawn me a picture of a rainbow, just as Tanya had shown me. I feel that was a gift from Tanya to me, maybe because of the friendship we had built up.

The other piece of important information I received from Tanya was that I was going to include her in my own book. For a long time I had been told I would share my knowledge of life after death, but the idea always ended up somewhere behind of the list of things I wanted to do and way behind everything I needed to do.

As I am writing this, I can't help but smile, my book is almost finished now and Tanya's story is one close to my heart and one I feel grateful I am able to share. Tanya showed me again, that the love between mother and child never dies. Ana taught me that not all grief is a dark place, the love I felt from Tanya for her mother is indescribable, a beautiful young girl who knew she would cross over to the other world before she was able to marry or have her own children. Yet Tanya still made the most of her life, and she experienced the joy of her mother's marriage and the new birth to the family.

21 *Pamela*

Phone call From Heaven

I was living in Ramsgate in the UK when I received a desperate phone call from my Nana. It was confirmed, my aunt Pamela had cancer. My Nana cried on the phone as she explained to me all the details of her daughter's illness. As I listened to my Nanas tears fall, I knew that my aunt wasn't going to survive. I felt sadness overcome me and I knew what was coming next. My Nana asked me directly, "She will get through this won't she?" Although I knew in my heart she wouldn't, I found myself comforting my Nana and telling her how strong my aunty Pam was.

Pamela lived quite close to my Nana and she would go to my Nana's house every day, sometimes just to take a bit of shopping, sometimes just to sit and watch some TV with her. Pamela was always popping in. As I lived at my Nana's house on and off for many years I would see her daily. She was a good person, her and my Nana would sit and gossip, watch some TV, and then she would leave. Ever since a child Pamela was deaf in one ear, so she would often shout or sometimes she wouldn't hear me. She was the mother of Amanda and Kimberly, I was especially close to Amanda and I would often sleep at their house. I saw a lot of Pamela whilst sleeping at her house over the years.

The news of Pamela's illness hit everyone in the family very hard. Being in her early forty's and having breast cancer was just devastating to us all. I tried to be positive. I had to be positive for my mum, she was trying so hard to be strong, she was reading about all the people who successfully survived breast cancer. I would smile and agree that Pamela would surely be one of those success stories, but I think we all knew deep down that Pamela's story wasn't going to have such a happy ending, and sadly it wasn't. Finally, my aunt Pam gave up the fight and passed over to the Spirit world. My Nana's world came crashing down around her. Again, I felt helpless.

Some years later, I had a dream, a very vivid and clear dream. I was in a big old red English telephone box and I was on the phone to Pamela. She told me not to sign the deal I was about to sign the next day. She told me in detail about how much mess I was about to get myself into and how much money I would end up owing. I woke up very worried.

That morning I was about to sign with the banks for a personal loan. Then I was about to sign with the owner of a shop I wanted to run. I felt the banks had gone out of their way to accept me for the huge loan, and the owner was coming from quite far away. Everything was set up, how could I not go through with it now? I had it all planned out, and today was the day after a lot of hard work and worry, I would finally get the keys to my new shop. I was so excited about it, and I was quite annoyed with the dream. I knew it was real, I knew Pamela was warning me and telling me not to go ahead with the deal, yet I couldn't let so many people down at the last minute, plus I really wanted this shop.

As I walked to the bank that morning, I could feel Pamela walking with me. Yet I had such hopes for the shop, I thought maybe I could just take it as a warning and work harder to not get into the debt Pamela was warning me about. I kept thinking of the word free will, I had my own free will to create my own destiny. Yes, that was it.

I signed the paperwork and got my keys, I pushed Pamela's warning to the back of my mind and I opened the shop with all the hope in the world.

Two years later, after working all the hours God had given me, after maintaining my shop by giving readings in my lunch break and late at night after work. After reaching breaking point, after the entire nightmare that I fought so hard for, I finally shut the shop down, I had 10 euros in my pocket, that was the only money I had after two years of tears and struggles, I owed the exact amount Pamela had told me I would owe.

I don't believe in mistakes, I do believe in every bad choice we learn. Of course, I regret not acting on Pamela's advice. One of the most important things I have learnt is that Spirit are there to help us. They only want the best for us. Family and friends we have on the Other Side will come to our aid when they feel we are going off route on destiny's track, sometimes we can't see them or hear them and we often miss the many messages they send us and the many ways they try to help us. Yet even still, when the message is loud and clear, it's not always easy to trust them and to follow their guidance.

Ironically, in those dreadful two years I had the shop I asked Spirit for help many times. I was so desperate I reduced myself to levels I never thought I would see in myself. I almost begged Spirit to help me; of course, I was never helped in my shop. Why? I realize now because that shop was not a part of my destiny, had it succeeded, had it been the success it should have been I would not have moved forward and taken the steps to the life I have now. What Spirit did give me were many signs that I was not alone, they proved to me endlessly that they were with me giving me strength and they constantly tried to help me move away from the shop. Of course, I was kicking and fighting for the opposite, I wanted the shop to work, I wanted money in the till, and I wanted my loans paid off.

Once, I was told by Spirit to close the doors and return the keys. I wasn't happy about this and again ignored the advice, "Why tell me this, if I leave now I will owe loads of money," I cried. "Why not just help more people come in and spend?" I asked. Looking back, if I would have listened that day and not ignored the advice I didn't like, I would have owed only a fraction of what was to come later.

No matter how much we want something, if we are going in the wrong direction from our destiny then it will never work out. Spirit can give us strength and support but they can never help us with our destiny if we are not on the right path. That's why we sometimes see people do things and it works out for them, yet we may do something in a "better way," yet it doesn't work out for us. That is because it is not part of our destiny. The man who ran the shop before me had it for over thirty years, he made an entire living out of it, he bought a house, a car and other things with the profit he made. He was able to give himself and his wife a job and for a few years, he even gave his daughter a job. Yet, in less than two years, it was a financial disaster for me. The reason is clear. It was not part of my destiny. I was not supposed to work there for thirty years.

I often see it as driving a car, if you are driving in the wrong direction, you will come across many obstacles, you will be scared and maybe hurt, you may crash into other cars, putting others off route or injuring their journey. Most importantly, you will never see the signs that are guiding you to your correct destination as you are driving in the wrong direction; the signs are all behind you. Until you stop, by crashing or having a breakdown, or maybe realizing that no matter how much you want to use this road, it isn't the right one, until you make a U-turn, you will constantly drive in the wrong direction and you will never make it to anywhere.

Unfortunately, most people wait for a crash or a breakdown, or like me, for both, before they change directions, the I want, I want, I want, in us kicks in, plus there is the hope issue, where we just hope things will get better, the praying and the positive thinking that somehow we will get to our destination. Miracles, hope, prayers, false positive thinking, they all help fuel our engine.

Unfortunately, when reality kicks in its only after our crash or breakdown for most of us.

Life constantly brings us challenges, each one of us has problems and have to fight and learn to become stronger and have a better life. However, if every step forward takes you a step backwards, if you find each month you are back where you started, if you find that your problems are affecting you emotionally, if you really can't see the way forward maybe it's time to stop and do a U-turn. No matter how hard it appears at the time.

I learnt a lot from Pamela's message and even though it's not easy, even still it took me a long time to trust that Spirit seems to know best. It's still hard to let go of my wants and to flow with destiny, yet I feel finally I am learning. No matter how clever I may feel I am, sometimes I have to let go and trust. I have to trust that God knows more than I do.

22 *Xavier*

Life, Death and a Birth

I hadn't yet reached my shop when I felt the presence of a young Spirit man, he seemed eager to talk and told me I was going to give a reading for his mother. When I reach my shop his mother Lucia was waiting for me, she seemed just as impatient as her son did for the reading to begin. Like most readings I didn't know Lucia but the impatience of both her and her son must have rubbed onto me as no sooner had I sat down I said, "Your son has passed and he is here."

Xavier talked a lot, he showed me some lovely valid information, he was very creative and artistic, he was a lovely Spirit, and his main concern was his mother. He really wanted her to know he was happy and at peace, a message I receive repeatedly from Spirit. For his mother to believe me Xavier seemed to think the more private information and details he gave, the more his mother would believe he was at peace.

The reading was personal, it was heavy, yet at the same time, Xavier gave out some lovely validating details of his life and his death. He showed me he had not felt well, gone to bed and Lucia had found him dead the next morning.

Xavier told his mum the news that he was going to be an uncle soon, and he would be there at the hospital, he went as far to tell me he was going to prove to his mum he was there for the birth. Lucia asked me what I was thinking, "How?" How was Xavier going to prove to his mum he was at the hospital. When Lucia asked me, that was the point Xavier stopped communicating, he had been communicating for a while, so I wasn't sure if he was tired or I was tired. Both Lucia and I discussed possible ways her son could prove he was at the hospital for the new birth in his family. I gave out some vague ideas, maybe the doctor would be named Xavier, maybe they would play a song that has great significance, and to be honest I had no idea. I suggested that maybe it would be something that she had felt connected to him since his passing, she laughed at that and said, "Well, unless you turn up at the hospital I can't think what."

"You won't live another hour." Those were the words the doctor said to me, as he gave me a simple echo scan, "I have been here for nine hours," was my reply between cries. Nine hours, five doctors, two huge sick bags, passed out three times, everyone and anyone had prodded me. I was so sick I had been lying on the floor with my bottom in the air for four hours, and finally, I had a simple scan and was told I would die within the hour unless I had an emergency operation. Andres was given a huge file of paperwork to sign, a consent form. I laugh now and wonder who would read that when their wife has an hour to live.

The doctor did save my life, apparently, I had a tumour on an ovary that had grown so big it had broken and it was poisoning my blood, hence me being sick black liquid for hours. I wasn't sure if that was even possible, but I wasn't about to argue.

They removed my ovary, removed my tumour, and sewed me up. I was alive. I woke up from the theatre and was happy to be alive. I heard my husband in the theatre waiting room as they wheeled me out to him; he was talking to someone and when he saw me, he came rushing over to me.

Then I heard a voice shout very loudly, "No, not you, I don't believe it," I turned my head and saw Lucia. Her granddaughter was being born in the theatre room next to mine. Whilst Lucia had been waiting in the waiting room for the birth of her grandchild she had started talking to my husband, all the time looking around for the promised sign from her son, she hadn't heard or seen nothing. As Lucia sat chatting to my husband, she was unaware I was the one in the theatre. She was desperately hoping her son was there for the birth as he had said he would be, on seeing me she remembered what she had told me, "unless he sends me you," and here I was.

I was blessed enough to see the little girl and the family were on the same ward so Lucia came to see me on several occasions.

When Spirit wants to send a message, they can go to great lengths. Xavier didn't make me ill, he didn't give me a tumour so I would be in the hospital that day. However, nor did he pre-warn me of any near death illness I was about to have. I felt for a long time I could have been warned by Spirit, maybe not a burning bush or a flying Angel but some kind of warning I was ill. I don't know why I felt this, but it really upset me. Ok, I will admit it, I was more than upset, I was very pissed off. If Xavier and Spirit knew I was going to be in the hospital, near death, why hadn't they warned me?

I have learnt since then I needed that operation for many reasons, a layer of reasons that I now understand. One reason being at the time I was completely burnt out from working many hours and giving readings in between work. I was becoming a zombie and although those who loved me kept warning me to slow down, I did not intend to do so. Until I found myself sat in a hospital room for nine days and then lying in bed at home for several weeks. I am grateful for Doctor Naranjo for saving my life. If I was Xavier's message, then he also knew I was going to be saved. I am more than glad I could help him be a part of his message to his mother of his continuing life. The Spirit of Xavier taught me the strength and energy Spirit will use to give a simple message, so much hard work for a Spirit to tell their loved ones they are at peace and are still around.

23 *Mikel*

Till Death Do Us Part

Terry came to me with little expectations of the reading, although she will admit she was very nervous yet she didn't really expect much to come from our meeting. Still, she did come with an open mind. The Spirit of Mikel came through to me almost immediately, he showed me a long illness, yet also showed me his death eventually was due to cardio problems. The love I felt from Mikel for his wife Terry was strong and powerful.

Terry confirmed that Mikel had been her husband and had suffered from cancer for many years yet, although, it was his heart that eventually gave up on him. The thing that struck me with Mikel was his young age. Terry confirmed that her husband was only 34 when he died after he had suffered from cancer for nine years.

Mikel showed me how much he loved Terry. He spoke to me in detail about his two daughters, how not only was he still with them, but how he was aware of all the changes they had encountered since his death. He spoke to me about his youngest daughter and he then went on to tell me about a personal problem she was suffering with.

Terry, at this point was moved by the details I was recounting to her. Private and personal details that were being retold to her, not only was it confirmation that Mikel was still with her, but also that what was happening with her daughter was very real and serious enough for her Mikel to come from the Spirit world to discuss it.

One thing I will never forget about Mikel was he showed me a bunch of yellow flowers for his wife. It was symbolic of their anniversary and he wanted to give his wife a bunch of flowers, at the same time my room filled with the perfume of flowers. My entire room was alive with the smell of fresh flowers.

Mikel wanted Terry to know he was still with her, Terry asked me if Mikel would wait for her, and I heard him very clearly reply "for eternity," with this reply Terry became emotional. She told me how "for eternity," were the very words Mikel had always replied to her when she had asked him.

It touched me so much to see a husband and father so young. I understood the pain the family had been through whilst Mikel had been ill.

Mikel showed me clips of Terry's life, things she had done since his passing. It was Mikel's way of showing he was still around. He then showed me clearly a hot air balloon, I made no sense of it at all, and Terry didn't look like the kind of woman who took journeys in a hot air balloon. "I'm seeing something important with a balloon, I'm seeing a big air balloon." As soon as the words left my mouth, I saw Terry's expression change. She excitedly went on to tell me how on her 40th birthday her family had surprised her with a journey in a hot air balloon.

"Mikel was with you that day," I replied his message to her. Terry went on to explain to me how on that day she had felt his presence very strongly. She felt like a breeze was around her and a feeling of being gently hugged.

Mikel also showed me that on the day he died he also showed her a sign he was with her. Terry confirmed that the day he died, she was sitting alone holding both their wedding rings in her hands, she asked Mikel to help her explain to her two young daughters that daddy wasn't with them anymore. A bright light came in from the window, reflecting brightly from the two rings, she felt at peace with the light and felt that Mikel was with her, telling her it would be ok.

Mikel stepped back and I felt the Spirit of another man, he was showing me lots of plants and flowers, he passed with a heart attack not long ago. Terry confirmed her friend who was a gardener had passed with a heart attack not long ago. He only came through briefly and the message was not for Terry but for his own wife, he wanted to tell his wife, he was ok, he was still with her, and he knew what pain she was in, he obviously loved her very much. I thought it was very kind of Mikel to allow another Spirit to come through whilst he was communicating with his wife. Mikel obviously knew how important it was that loved ones are given the chance to receive a message from the Other Side.

The gardener told me his family was going to hold some type of get together soon in his name, in the countryside, and he would be there.

Terry confirmed that his family were having a reunion that Saturday and they all planned a day out in the country where they were going to plant a tree in his honour.

This Spirit told me quite clearly that it wasn't to be this Saturday. Terry was slightly taken aback and claimed it was. The gardener was sure it wasn't and Terry was adamant the reunion was on Saturday. It was actually quite an amusing moment. I felt the Spirit man laughing yet he was obviously going to prove his point.

I asked Terry is there any way she could confirm the day of the reunion, explaining that I had a feeling the Spirit man was probably right. Terry worked out some dates and she realized for the first time that the date didn't fall on a Saturday, instead, it was on a Sunday. We both laughed together as it was confirmed that he was right about the date in which he was going to have a tree planted in his honour.

Mikel then returned. He wanted me to repeat to Terry that he wanted her to be happy and enjoy her life. He told me that she would meet somebody else one day that she wasn't to feel guilty or to stop her feelings for someone new because she still loved him. Mikel told me that in the Spirit world they don't have marriage as we do in our physical world. When you die, you return to the arms of love, if you have more than one marriage. You don't have to choose, there is no jealousy in the Spirit world. When we pass, we meet up with all our Spirit family, all our husbands or wives; we feel the same love as we did before our parting. We are able to reunite, and if there is more than one partner, then we are able to share that love just as equally, without jealousy, just the pure love we feel in our hearts.

Mikel made it clear that when Terry loves again, he would be happy for her, he would be there to celebrate it with her, and although he loved her dearly, he didn't want her to spend her life a lonely person, he wanted her to feel love and to be loved again. She could find love a thousand times, yet he would still be there waiting for her for eternity.

Mikel's message has echoed through Spirit messages over the years to me. It seems we can have a hundred marriages and when we pass over, then we can meet with them all, and we are able to be part of their life in Spirit. The love will still flow and we can still grow as partners. I feel like Mikel's message is important.

I have met many people who were very much in love when their partner died, and some want to move on, some are scared to move on and others actually feel guilty about moving on and having another romance, feeling like it somehow takes away the love they felt for their partners.

How long it long enough, how much time are you supposed to wait before you move on and find another relationship after your partner dies? If you are in love, then the time it takes for you to move forward should really make little difference, a day or maybe a decade, it will make little difference in the sense that you will still love your partner who has passed. Time will not help you fall out of love. Instead, I know that our loved ones, more than anything want us to enjoy our life, to continue to feel loved and to continue to live a full life. When we die we will all reunite and no matter how many partners or marriages, we have experienced, we will reunite in a loving way with them all, but until then, till death do us part.

24 Kelvin

An Ocean Of White Flowers

When I first met Kelvins mum, I was struck by her beauty and her stunning piercing blue eyes. A little boy came to communicate with me and with tears in her eyes; Monica confirmed her son had passed. Kelvin communicated to me very fast and with a huge amount of detail, he told me many personal, significant details about his short life and he told me about many changes his mum had made since his passing. Kelvin and his family had lived in Germany when he was diagnosed with cancer and sadly, he died in Germany. Monica is Spanish and now lived back in Spain and had been able to reconstruct her life, and although she had since remarried and had other children, Kelvin was still missed very much.

Kelvin was aware of his mother's changes, he had been walking with her since his passing. Some of the details Kelvin showed me were precious; his mother still had his favourite teddy on her bedside table and how he played with his little stepbrothers. Kelvin spoke about things that had happened in the hospital whilst he was ill and he even spoke about his funeral.

Any mother and child reunion is heart wrenching for me, and although I was feeling Monica's pain I was amazed by the communication Kelvin was giving. He laughed and even made jest of certain situations that had happened with him and Monica. Kelvin touched on the subject of his father and I felt Monica was receiving a huge amount of healing that day.

Kelvin told me he was now working to help other children with cancer, to be with them whilst they die or to be with them until their recovery so as they wouldn't feel lonely. Everything Kelvin was telling me or showing me I was repeating to Monica as fast as I could. This one piece of information really stood out for me, to be with them whilst they die or until they recover, Kelvin was there to help, to play with them and stop any loneliness. I continued giving his messages and Monica thanked me so much on leaving.

A few weeks later, I was in my bedroom when two things happened to me at once. First, I saw Kelvin sat in my bedroom, just as I looked at him my phone rang. It happened simultaneously and for a moment, I didn't know whether to speak to the Spirit child or answer the phone.

Instinct told me to answer the phone.

It was a Spanish woman who lived in Germany, she had been given my number from a friend who had been on holiday to Spain and had a reading from me.

Her son was in the hospital, a young boy the same age as Kelvin. She wanted to ask me if I could see if he was going to die or not. Although he had been diagnosed with cancer and the doctors had said there wasn't much more they could do for him, she cried on the phone as she asked me if there was any way I could help.

I told her clearly that unfortunately I could not help. I told her there was nothing physically I could do and nothing on a spiritual level I could do. All I could do was pray she found strength in this hard time; at that point, I turned around and saw Kelvin again. I had completely forgotten about him.

Then the words just came to me. I told the woman on the phone that I couldn't tell if her son was to live or die, that wasn't information I had, but what I did know was that while she was away from the hospital room, there was a little Spirit boy who goes and plays with her son. I explained about Kelvin and his work helping other children who were suffering from cancer. I looked at Kelvin and saw him smile as I told the woman, "Your son is not alone when you are not there."

I couldn't believe the response, the lady was almost jumping down the phone to kiss me, she explained to me that she had several other children, no family, and little money, she often had to leave her sick son on his own in the hospital to run home and look after her other children. A horror story for anybody and more so a mother.

One of her prayers was that her son did not feel alone whilst she had to run home and do mundane chores to keep her other children fed and safe. She was elated just knowing he had a Spirit friend to play with.

She kept thanking me, telling me that it may sound silly, but to her it made a huge difference.

I could still see Kelvin in my bedroom. He wasn't just smiling now, he was laughing, and then he left.

When I hung up the phone, I silently thanked Kelvin, I don't know how I could have helped the woman if Kelvin hadn't appeared and I hadn't remembered his words about him helping other children.

I decided to thank Kelvin for his kindness at helping other children and helping me with the phone call. I had a thought about white flowers and throwing them into the sea as a sign of thanks for him. It was something I had never done before and the thought wouldn't leave my mind.

On the Monday, I missed the flower shop, on the Tuesday, there were no white flowers in the flower shop. On the Wednesday, it was shut. On the Thursday, I was too busy. On the Friday, I was determined this would be the day, and I suddenly had a startling thought. I had a garden in my apartment block, it was blooming with white flowers, I had been walking past them every day, yet I had not realized.

I took a pair of scissors and walked down to the garden, I was going to cut a few flowers as to not get in trouble with the gardener and then go to the beach. When I got downstairs, I heard someone hiss me, I turned around to find the gardener with a bunch of white flowers. "Would you like a few of these, they have just been cut?" she asked me. I am still amazed at how Spirit work.

I walked down to the beach with my fresh cut white flowers, it was a hot August day and I wanted to find a quiet spot so I walked down some way as the beach was still quite busy. As I got further down I saw the perfect place, there were a few people around but not many. Just as I stepped onto the sand, I saw Monica, my jaw almost dropped open when not only did I see Monica standing in front of me but she was also holding a bunch of white flowers.

We both asked at the same time, "What are you doing here?" Monica answered first and explained to me it was Kelvin's anniversary, each year as she can't return to Germany to lay flowers for him, she throws white flowers into the sea, symbolizing that the water will take the flowers to him. I couldn't believe how we had met on the beach this way. I had somehow become part of Kelvin and his mother's special anniversary moment.

Talking to Monica whilst still on the beach we touched on the subject of music. I explained that sometimes Spirit will work it in such a way that a special song is played at just the right moment, its Spirits way of showing us they are still with us, music can be magical. On the way home from the beach, a Native American Indian started playing the song we played at my dad's funeral. The Native Indian played songs every night, not only did I know all his songs I also had his CD, he had never played my dad's song before, and he never played it since.

I will never forget Kelvin and the power of a Spirit child.

The woman from Germany phoned me back quite some time later, at first, I didn't recognize her voice until she explained who she was. Unexpectedly to her and the doctors, her son had made a full recovery and was now at home. I cried with happiness when we finished talking.

25 Antonio

Duty Call

I don't believe in mediums being a substitute for grief and I am against dependency on a medium for grief therapy. In fact, something as wonderful as communicating with a loved one through a medium can become very negative if it becomes a need, a dependency. So far, I have never had this problem with people, I simply explain the process, and of course, Spirit would not turn up each time if I had the same client and they needed repeat reassurance.

Antonio was a special exception for me. I first met the Spirit of Antonio when his daughter had come to me for a reading. Over the years, Pilli came back for a reading around twice or three times a year. The one thing that always surprised me was that her father usually came through with a message, I still haven't completely understood why, but I have never had the same Spirit appear so often in a reading. Thankfully, his messages were always new and different and often they didn't involve Pilli at all. Pilli wasn't dependent on the messages from her father, yet she did feel the warmth from them.

Antonio had been a police officer in life, a good husband and a good man, Pilli loved her father dearly. When he died, she had been devastated and within two years, her mother went home to Spirit with her father.

I was more amazed by the things Antonio would tell me than the fact that he always appeared in a reading. He told me he had chosen to help on the Other Side, to be a worker. He would go to disaster sites and worldwide events wherever there was help needed. Once he told me he wouldn't be around for a while, he had a big event to deal with in Haiti. Shortly afterwards the country was hit by an earthquake. Another time he told me he had to go as he was preparing for a plane crashing, the next morning I woke to the news of a plane crash. Antonio always wanted to tell his daughter, he was still around her, although he often seemed to be in a rush, always working, much like in life.

He would give me small yet amazing pieces of information about his life in the Afterlife. I was happy to know more about the Other Side.

Antonio told me an amazing thing once. I was giving a reading for Pilli and suddenly he just seemed to appear to me. He told me to tell his daughter, he was still with her when she needed him and he was happy and loved her still very much. Then he told me he was on holiday, yes on holiday, I couldn't believe what I was hearing. It was the first time I had ever heard of Spirits being on holiday, out of curiosity, I couldn't wait to ask where his holiday destination was. Antonio told me he was on holiday with his wife in Egypt.

For some reason Spirits working didn't surprise me as much as Spirits taking holidays. Since then I have heard about spiritual holidays by numerous Spirits and it brings home to me just how wonderful the Spirit world really is.

Over the years, I met Antonio quite a few times and he often showed me a different aspect of the Spirit world that I hadn't known previously. He always seemed such a busy person, watching over his family still living, yet working hard in the Spirit world to bring as much peace to disasters as possible, and yet he still took his holidays and was able to dance with his wife.

Once I was so tired and so fed up of working. I felt like I could go to bed for a month and not wake up. I remember thinking to myself, if I have to work when I pass over to the Other Side then I'm not going, but it was explained to me that all work was voluntary and it was all done based on love and not physical energy, it was giving healing and peace, and it was not tiresome. It was about giving and helping.

During one of my early readings with Pilli, she asked her father what it was like on the Other Side. Antonio replied to his daughter, "The most beautiful bliss, you could ever imagine. A single flower can have you in awe for moments that are lost in time. A peace so great no human feeling can describe it. A love so pure and a happiness that is so grand you spread it around. A family life so huge you realize how we are all connected. We have fun like you have never known, we laugh with such laughter that you would never understand. We have the best parties, the best reunions and the best music."

He then continued "Halls and halls for studying, huge buildings where we work to help you find treatments and new inventions, before you receive any good idea in your world, we have long thought it here. Your world is just a dull reflection of ours, here we are more alive and more active than you are, you are on a mere holiday compared to our active lives."

I built up a good friendship with Antonio over the years and I have got to know his wife Carmen since, who is with him on the Other Side. For a long time now I haven't given a reading for Pilli, there is no need, also I now consider her more as a friend. She has found her peace with her parents passing and I feel she wants them to enjoy their life, after life.

I do sometimes talk with Antonio, private little conversations where he has shown me more about his life on the Other Side. The last time I saw him I had to laugh, he told me he had to go because he was on duty call.

I will always thank Antonio for the glimpses of the Other Side that he continues to show me, some things like holidays in Egypt was new and interesting.

26 Adolfo

A Return Flight Home

Another hot sunny day on the Costa Blanca, when a lady from Bilbao named Silvia came to me for a reading. To me, she was just another reading yet as soon as she sat down, I felt such pressure and a tightening around my throat I started to physically cough. I was feeling the Spirit of Adolfo.

Adolfo showed me he had been a very good-looking man who had suffered from depression. He showed me cancer and showed me he had not wanted his family to suffer with his illness. Adolfo had been a heavy smoker and was convinced his lungs had been badly affected. His own depression, the fear of becoming ill, and having to depend on his family had increasingly made his mind very troubled.

On the 22nd of December, Adolfo decided that he wanted to leave this world behind, and in one of the most saddest actions, he hung himself.

The first message Adolfo wanted me to repeat to his wife Silvia was how sorry he was that he put his family through so much pain. He had three sons and a daughter and he showed me clearly how he had witnessed the pain he had caused due to taking his own life. He loved his family dearly and he apologized for the pain and the devastating effects he left behind. I could feel the emotions flowing through Silvia as her husband passed on his messages through me. He also told me since his passing, he had been visiting Silvia and his children often, still participating in his family. He was still very much around his family and was up to date with everything that had happened since his passing.

Adolfo was sorry for the pain he caused by taking his own life, he obviously loved his family dearly and talked about his grandchildren and how he took much joy from being around them and how proud he was of his children.

However, he explained how he had felt his death was necessary for him. He needed his peace and felt his own death was the only way to end his inner tortures. On passing and seeing the effect he left behind, I felt he was truly sorry for the hurt and tears he caused.

He told me he wanted Silvia, to continue to enjoy her life, he wanted her to go out and play, enjoy every day of her life in a way he was unable to do.

Adolfo confirmed to me something I had heard many times from Spirits who had taken their own lives, death and the process of returning home to Spirit is the same for everyone. Because he took his own life didn't send him into any dark hole or any empty place for lost souls, he was also met by his Spirit family. He entered into the Spirit world just as any other Spirit does. There was no difference when he left his physical body due to his own actions than if he would have died a natural death. He wasn't lost or wandering around.

Yet what Adolfo did express to me was that he still had to go through a process, he had to see his own life and the effects he had left behind. Of course taking his own life suggested that the effect had been very dramatic, although Adolfo had now found his peace, and he was surrounded in love and light, he still had to face his own effects and had to deal with his issues and his own healing. He had worked on himself and I felt his presence in the reading to express to his wife how sorry he was, was part of his own healing. I had no doubt Adolfo was a happy and peaceful Spirit, yet it proved again to me that suicide is never the solution, the healing still has to be found if not on this side than on the Other Side. The inner work is still the same. Suicide is not a way out.

Adolfo echoed to me a message I have heard several times from Spirit.

Real home is the spiritual home, earthly life is just a journey, and it's a holiday. We come to this world to enjoy our holiday. It's compared to a visit to another country. It's a journey to learn, to love, and to enjoy. It's a physical journey combined with our spiritual and emotional journey. It's a journey also of touch and of new experiences.

The physical world is a mere reflection of the magic of the Spirit world, our real home.

The nine months we grow in the womb of our mother is our time for forgetting our spiritual home. It's a time of physical growth, each toenail, each cell, each layer of skin all grown as to enter the physical world. We are born dependent on our mothers to feed us whilst in the womb and for her to protect us the best she can.

Our mother depends on external resources for her own survival and ours. We are born completely dependent on resources such as air, food and water. Before starting this journey, before entering the womb of our mother we had no such need, neither air, water or food are needed for our spiritual body's.

Depending on such external resources as living humans, we should be protecting our environment, it's a holiday we should want to leave as clean as we can, and knowing many other generations will want to come for future holidays makes it all the more important.

Apart from the enjoyment of touch, of sex, of physical enjoyment, we are here to share love, and to enjoy, to really enjoy. To have fun, to experience complete joy.

Unfortunately, some people don't enjoy this holiday, instead, they believe they got off the plane at the wrong stop. They talk about how much better it should be, how other people seem to have better hotel rooms, and how we received a bad deal on this holiday. Some people seemed to be placed in the worse resorts.

Of course we arrive with a tour guide, a guide who is on call night and day, a guide who if we asked would show us the easiest routes of our holiday, unfortunately, many don't realize they arrive here with their own personal tour guide.

We reunite with many of our Spirit family, family and friends who have been on many journeys with us, they choose to come back with us and share this holiday. Taking on different forms as our parents, family, spouses, and friends. Most people forget to recognize their Spirit family. The time we spend in the womb helps us to forget, allowing us to enjoy an entirely new relationship with them.

We will at some point feel most human emotions, tasting the wines of the country, but we will eventually all return home. We will all remember again and we will have photographs and memories stored in our souls.

Unfortunately for some people, like Adolfo, some have the burning desire to return home before the return flight is booked, and although he took the quick route home, he still had to resolve the issues he had left behind. Suicide won't leave a Spirit out in the cold, but it will never solve the issues that made them take that path to start with.

I felt Adolfo had confronted his issues and had now found his healing. He spoke to me about love and about happiness, and he was still around his family when he chose to be.

He still loved his wife dearly. He wanted his wife to enjoy her life to the fullest, not to miss a moment of her own journey. To move on from his death and instead dance for them both, sing so he could hear her and laugh so he could feel her happiness.

Adolfo reminded me of the sad reality that this world can be hard and overwhelming. How even with the best wife and the loveliest children, we can still see a black hole surrounding us. Adolfo also reminded me that suicide is never the answer no matter how it may seem like the only solution at the time; it is neither a solution nor an answer to our inner turmoil or external problem.

One day in the distant future, Adolfo showed me he would be reunited with his wife and family, and he would take another journey back here to the physical world, I hope he has a happier time next time.

27 Juan

Soul Sisters

Spirits don't often predict the future nor do they often give out warnings. I guess their reason for communicating is to be able to show their loved ones they are still around and that love still lives on. In the case of Antonia, even I was surprised with her reading and the message she received from her husband Juan, who had passed over to cancer some years previous.

Antonia had come to me for a reading having had a stranger suggest a reading may cheer her up. Antonia had been feeling quite lonely and hopeless and thought she would, "give me a go," as she described it.

Her husband Juan came through and although I could feel the message of love I also felt slightly agitated. I felt it was he who was slightly agitated as if he wanted to tell me something of importance and it wasn't just a message of love for his wife. I briefly closed my eyes and tried to find silence and clarity. Antonia was an elderly woman and at this point, she was just staring at me with an intrigued look. Juan had told her some information that was accurate, but I had to keep stopping, as I felt so agitated. This feeling was messing up my reading and that's why I took a moment to calm down. As I found my silence, I was able to connect more clearly with Juan. His message was serious as he told me Antonia had to go and see her sister.

I repeated the message to Antonia, trying to tone down the urgency of it and not to scare her, "Juan feels you should go and see your sister," I said. Of course, no matter how I tried to tone it down Antonia was still startled and asked me why.

"Because she is going to need you," I replied to her, repeating her husband's message. Antonia was quiet for a moment and then she asked me, "When should I go and see her?" I had a feeling that Antonia's sister lived quite far away and yet Juan didn't seem to see that as a problem when I heard him say, "Now."

"I feel your sister is going to need you now," I said, realizing I was not doing very well at toning down the message. Antonia was quite worried and I hated seeing people come to me for a reading and leaving more concerned than when they arrived. My job was to bring peace, understanding and communication from the Spirit world, not to bring fear and warnings.

Juan continued with his messages to his wife, mostly of love and laughter, and I felt the agitation leave him and Antonia was happy with her messages from her husband. She had been very lonely since his death. She had no family close by and she often went days without speaking to a soul. She told me some days the only conversation she had was when she went to buy the bread in the morning. This reminded me of an elderly man I met whilst working in the shop, he had started to talk to me about the weather and then we had a general conversation about something trivial, on leaving he smiled at me and thanked me. He told me I was most likely going to be the only person he spoke to that day, as he had no family and lived alone.

Antonia was much the same, she would go for her bread in the morning, have a brief conversation with the woman in the bread shop then return home and spend the rest of her day in her own silence. Her days since her husband's death had been sad.

It was almost a year after the reading when I saw Antonia again. She told me the story of what happened after our last meeting.

She had returned home that evening and thought about the messages from her husband. She knew Juan worried about her all the time when he was alive, she wondered why he would tell her to go and see her sister? Her sister Marie lived an eight-hour train journey away, although she was very close to her sister, she normally only visited once a year as Antonia wasn't a good traveller.

That evening she couldn't seem to settle, she wondered if Juan had shown her so much proof he was around her, surely she should listen to his message about her sister needing her, but she also wondered why her sister needed her. Antonia made her mind up. She packed a small bag, locked her door and headed for the train station. She told me she had never done anything so spur of the moment before. There was a part of her, telling her she wasn't young enough to be jumping on a train and visiting family without informing them first, yet at the same time she trusted Juan had really communicated with her during the reading, surely he wouldn't have said what he said for no reason.

Antonia travelled throughout the night, again, something she had never done before. Finally, after an eight-hour journey, she arrived at her destination at 9 am. From the train station, she took a taxi to her sister's house, she had never travelled alone and wasn't quite sure how to arrive.

As the taxi arrived at her sister's address, Antonia saw the scene that was happening before her, and after following the message given by her husband and travelling throughout the night, she realized why she was there.

Outside her sister's home was an ambulance. The ambulance men were taking her brother in law on a stretcher to the hospital, he had suffered a heart attack. Marie was sobbing behind the stretcher and clearly in shock when she turned to the taxi that pulled up by her side only to find her sister was the passenger. Antonia had the taxi driver follow the ambulance to the hospital and there they were able to hug. Antonia was with her sister each moment during the critical hours while her brother in law was fighting for his life. Marie couldn't believe how her sister had turned up out of the blue just at the moment she most needed someone, and as the doctors told Marie that sadly it was over, her husband lost his fight, his heart attack had been fatal and he had passed away in the emergency room. It was Antonia's arms she fell into.

Antonia stayed with her sister for many months after the death of her brother in law. She helped her in all the grief she had previously had to suffer herself. She was able to cry with her sister, laugh with her, and bring light to the darkness. Antonia told me that each day they would talk about my reading and how the message from Juan had changed her life.

Both Antonia and Marie, who had now seemed to appear from nowhere, hugged me and thanked me and told me to continue with my work. As I watched the two sisters walking off I suddenly realized how a year earlier, I had given a message from Spirit that was able to change the lives of two women. I wished the message had been one where I was able to save the brother in law from a fatal heart attack and yet I knew that is not the way life and death worked.

I feel Juan had wanted his wife to be with her sister at the hard time, both sisters have hardly been apart since, both making regular visits to each other's homes, looking after each other and living through the tears of grief together. Juan knew that by sending Antonia to Marie's at that time would make Antonia become part of her sister's journey. Antonia was able to cook for Marie, keep her home and clothes clean and Marie didn't have to suffer the weeks after her husband's death of being home alone.

What seemed to me like a bit of a harsh message at first and I was hesitant to pass it on, turned out to be as always, the correct message.

28 Rick

One for the Road

Rick was my mum's third husband, she married him when I was nineteen so he was a huge part of my life and played a good role as my stepdad, he was also a good friend.

Rick was a good man, an honest, law abiding, kind hearted, fun man. Although I was prepared for his illness due to bad dreams I had been having about him taking ill and dying, I was still not prepared for losing him. I had to watch my mum's transformation throughout Rick's illness. She became his life force, his nurse and ultimately his widow.

Rick had worked all his life in good jobs, from the army to the police force. He worked his way up to Scotland Yard and then worked with the anti-terrorist squad. On his retirement, he and my mum moved to Spain to be closer to my children and me and to enjoy the life of sun, sea and sangria.

Having enjoyed just a couple of years in Spain, Rick became ill. Having to return to England for treatment was the end of a dream for both him and my mum. I took flights back to the UK to see him and to be some kind of support for my mum throughout his illness; it was saddening each time I had to return home to Spain. Each time leaving him weaker and weaker.

I had only been back to Spain for a week since my last visit when I received a phone call from my mum informing me Ricks life was now coming to an end. I took the next flight back. I arrived late evening and Rick was asleep, a special bed had been set up in the living room for him.

Ricks children and his father were all staying at my mum and Rick's home, all broken hearted. That night my mum held her loving husband's hand. They were still so much in love. They still had so many dreams they wanted to live, she held his hand and as tears rolled down her face, she whispered to him, "Go on love, your mum will be waiting for you, go to your mum now. I'm going to be fine." Rick heard her words; he smiled and took his last breath.

The following night mum and I, along with Rick's daughter Leah were in bed together. Leah was like a sister to me. I had just woken from a dream where I had seen Rick on the beach. He was dressed in a white suit and he appeared healthy and happy again. As I woke my mum shouted, "Can you see that," I opened my eyes and saw a small blue ball of light, it had what appeared to be a black tail. It spun around the room for some time whilst we all lay in bed watching it and then it twirled and left through the door. My mum said, "That was Rick." She took great comfort from the blue twirling ball of light.

For some reason, neither my mum nor I dreamed or felt Rick's presence for a long time. As a working medium, I was talking to Spirits on a daily basis and I often wondered why I never felt Rick around me. People assume with me talking to Spirit all day that I can talk to whoever I choose, especially my own family. Unfortunately, it doesn't work that way. I can only speak to the Spirits that come to me.

It was several years later when mum and I were in Benidorm. It was Rick's birthday and we always did something special. Normally we would go out for Spanish tapas, order his favourite chipirones, (small fried squid), and spend the night with a bottle of wine recounting old memories of when he was still alive.

This time in Benidorm, we decided to go to a cheap and horrid Chinese where we had eaten there with Rick the first time we had all gone to Benidorm together. After the Chinese, we ended up walking past an Irish bar. Rick loved Irish bars so we thought it would be a good idea to go in for a drink.

That night each song that played in the bar was a song that Rick loved or he had bought for my mum. It was quite amazing as the music blasted in our ears we were almost transported back to the time we would listen to the songs when he was still alive.

Although the magic of the music was in some way comforting us, the barman stole the night. When he came from around the bar it was the first time we actually noticed him. He had the same bald head and big ears as Rick, he even stood like Rick and he said his name was Ricky.

My mum and I both looked at each other and laughed at the coincidence, then Ricky announced he had a special birthday request for someone in the bar, everyone then sang happy birthday. Me and my mum both looked up and together we sang happy birthday to Rick. That night we felt Rick's presence with us, through music, through a man who resembled him and through all the "coincidences" of the night. It was a truly special night.

The following year we decided to return to the same horrid Chinese and on the way home, we thought it would be nice to return to the same Irish bar. First, we stopped at a cabaret bar where there was a Rod Stuart lookalike on. My mum loves Rod and Rick had bought her all his albums. We listened to a few songs and then Rod announced a special birthday, and again we were able to sing "Happy Birthday" to Rick. After we left Rod, we walked to the Irish bar, only to find it was in darkness. "Oh, never mind," we said to each other, and walked on.

My mum had just asked me why she doesn't dream of Rick often. I didn't either, but I told her he most probably does go to her in her dreams, she just doesn't remember, plus I reminded her that she hardly ever sleeps long enough to dream. My mum is a big cat napper; she will doze off and then be wide-awake again for hours. In fact, I am unsure if she ever really sleeps at all.

On walking past the Irish bar, we saw Ricky sitting outside in darkness, again, I had to laugh at the resemblance he had of Rick, he stood up and started talking to us, apologising for closing the Irish bar relatively early.

"No problem," my mum said to him as we were about to walk away. He then gently touched my mum's arm and whispered, "I'll see you in your dreams," and winked, and then he then turned and walked inside. My mum and I just stood for a moment quite shocked. We wondered why he had said those words. Whatever his reason for saying "I'll see you in your dreams," makes no difference, he most likely says it to all the ladies, but to us, it was the comfort we both needed.

I honestly believe Spirit had staged the entire night, and the previous year. Spirit use these simple yet magical ways to tell us that they are still by our side. Songs of significance, a special birthday request, strange conversations with strangers, are all ways Spirit communicate. Me and my mum both felt comfort and appreciation with all we received on Rick's birthday. Yes, I would love to be able to talk to him as I do with other Spirits when I give a reading, but maybe I am not ready.

Rick and I always had a joke after a meal or if I were just having a drink with him, we would say, "One for the road," and have the last drink. Often we would laugh and after four or five more, we would still be saying, "One for the road," often adding, "Well it's a long road."

I often have a drink, put my glass up, and say to him, "One for the road," I miss him dearly.

.

29 Patrick

Irish Eyes

It was a warm sunny day and I had been standing outside the shop where I was working on Benidorm seafront. I often stood outside between readings and watched the gentle waves of the deep blue Mediterranean sea as they gently played with the sand, the light blue sky reaching down to the horizon of the deep blue sea, creating what appeared like a perfect straight line separating the two shades of blue. I felt almost hypnotized by the beauty of nature. I knew how lucky I was to work in such peaceful surroundings.

After admiring the same yet ever changing view, I returned to my room inside the shop, a lovely room that had been created only for the soul purpose of being a reading room. As I was the only one who worked in the shop as a reader, I had decorated the room to my own liking, I would often sit quietly and meditate in there.

I was contemplating meditating when a Spanish woman appeared by the door, as she sat down I asked her name and she told me she was called Ines.

I have met many people in my life, but I don't ever remember meeting a person who transmitted to me so much peace and kindness as Ines, her eyes were so calming yet her smile lit up my room.

Although Ines was Spanish, she had lived in Ireland for many years with her family and her husband Patrick, an Irish man from Dublin who had passed to Spirit some four years previous. Patrick communicated to me loud and clear. I felt so comfortable with Patrick; I felt a fun and happy character with him. I knew instantly that Patrick was a family man who, after almost a lifetime with his wife, died still very much in love with her.

His messages to his wife Ines were almost immediate. He came to tell her how much he still loved her, how he was still very much involved in the family since his passing and how much he loved his family. Patrick gave me many personal and small details about his life and his family, of course, to anyone it may seem small details, to his wife it was all significant confirmation that he was with her.

He was a man who enjoyed life, he showed me lots of laughter, he showed me music, and I felt I personally knew him before the end of the reading. He was only 66 when he died, he was still full of life and I feel Patrick was such a happy Spirit, because he had been able to enjoy so much love in his lifetime.

Patrick showed me his love for Ireland and then he also showed me a small gold cross, this was the only information Ines could not understand at the time, but Patrick kept showing it to me repeatedly. I felt like I was looking at a small picture of a gold cross.

Patrick told me his anniversary was in April, and I saw a huge bunch of yellow flowers for Ines, he said she would receive yellow flowers from him come April.

Ines told me that Patrick had planted hundreds of bulbs of yellow daffodils, in April they should all be blooming. Many months later, I heard from Ines and her yellow flowers had bloomed that year like no other year previously.

Patrick seemed more serious when he told me to tell Ines when she dies, whenever that time shall be, he would be there to take her home with him. He really wanted me to repeat these words, "When she dies I will be the one to take her home." Even though it sounded morbid, I felt the urge to repeat what I was hearing word for word.

Little did I know, for Ines this was the most important message of the reading, Ines told me how every day since Patrick had passed, she has spoken to him, always asking the same thing, "When I go, please come for me." I felt quite emotional myself hearing this.

Ines said she felt so much peace knowing that when her time eventually comes, he will be the one to take her home.

Patrick spoke for a while, but it was as our reading was ending that he told me he would continue to show Ines he was with her by sending her feathers in a special way, not just a feather from a bird flying past.

As Ines was leaving, she took out Patrick's small funeral card to show it to me, and there we saw the little cross he had been showing me, I thought that was another lovely confirmation for Ines.

I saw Ines shortly after the reading. She excitedly told me how a feather had mysteriously appeared by her window, not| long afterwards more feathers started to appear in strange and unusual places. I thought it was interesting; I hadn't really been too sure how much I believed a feather was a message from Spirit. Yet I did remember a few times in my life when I needed a sign from Spirit, I had found a feather and taken it to be a sign from my loved one that they were still with me. Although I was also conscious at the time I found a feather that I had desperately needed a sign, and any sign would have helped me. Therefore, I was slightly dubious about Spirits intervention of placing feathers in strange places, even knowing how capable spirit are of sending signs in all manner of ways.

I saw Ines a few weeks later and she told me I should write a book, I explained to her that I already was, she smiled at me and softly said I should finish it. Her words were spoken softly, with a smile, but I felt an electric bolt shoot through my body. My dream for years had been to finish my book.

The morning after my conversation with Ines I went for my morning coffee with my husband, in a friendly Irish bar on Benidorm seafront where we had become regulars. On this particular morning, it was a wet and grey day, the light blue sky and the deep blue sea I had been privileged to see on a daily basis was instead, today a dull shade of grey, and yet I was very excited as I ordered my coffee. I sat and told my husband about my conversation with Ines and how I was going to concentrate on my book. Andres was only half-awake and appeared only half-interested, but still I excitedly told him how I was convinced I wanted to put Patrick in my book and how I would explain his "feathers from Heaven." My husband smiled at me and replied that he thought it was a good idea. I wasn't really sure how interested he was in my book or even if he had any idea what it was really about.

My coffee was burning hot and I decided to concentrate on it for a while, I gently blew into the cup in the hope to cool it down. The more I gently blew into the cup, the more I became aware of my breathing and I felt my body relax and take on a different beat. My mind wandered as I continued blowing and suddenly I felt myself fall into a slightly more relaxed state. "Will I ever finish my book?" I wondered to myself. I was quite excited about my new chapter. As I started to return to my normal breathing, I whispered to myself, "Am I supposed to write this book?" with that, I was brought back to my surroundings. I realized I had wandered off somewhere in my mind. I was still in a conversation with Andres about the chapter of Patrick and my coffee was now cold. I sat up and began to drink my coffee when something caught my eye, right in front of my eyes, was a small white feather, it was just gently floating from mid-air down to my feet. I watched in amazement as the feather floated from side to side, almost dancing before my eyes until it landed by my feet.

I picked up the feather and put it in my purse, for some reason I knew it was Patrick. I could feel his presence, I felt like I wanted to give this feather to Ines, but how?

Later that day, due to an unrelated issue I ended up at Ines home, a beautiful home that transmits just as much peace as the lady herself. I sat at her dining room table with the sun gently warming my skin and the sea view almost hypnotizing me. I finally got onto the subject of the feather and I was just about to explain my story of my morning feather when Ines showed me her wall unit. Inside her large white wall unit, she had a small picture frame, and in the frame were all the feathers that Ines had found in "strange" circumstances since Patrick's visit with me.

I gave her my feather for her collection and Ines placed it in the frame with her other feathers. Ines was due to return back to Ireland soon and I felt sad that she was leaving. By now, we had built up a friendship. I always felt happy on seeing her and I enjoyed our conversations. Although I knew, she would be back soon.

The magic of my morning feather slowly eased off and almost forgotten and over the next few months so was my book. I found myself with no free time to write and again it had become nothing more than a forgotten dream. There were only two things keeping my idea of writing a book alive, one was the inner desire I had to reach as many people as I could to share the many magical moments I had with Spirit, and the other thing was my mother. She would constantly slip in the question, "When are you going to finish your book?" whenever she could. She would even try to disguise her question by changing her tactic, "Wow, that's amazing, you should put that in a book."

However, I still couldn't find the time. One day I went to bed for my siesta, although it was supposed to have been a quick catnap before returning to work, It ended up being a three-hour long sleep where I had a very vivid dream.

I dreamt that I was talking to Spirit and Spirit told me to share my knowledge. The dream was very real, but on waking, I wondered what knowledge I was to share? I didn't think I had any knowledge other then everything I know about Spirit and the Spirit world. That was the only thing I knew about that I could share, my thoughts returned to my book. "Ok," I said out loud, "I need to clear this up, if you feel I should write, send me a sign, a real clear sign. Send me a very strange feather." I laughed again at my own silliness and out loud, I said, "Or I will make it simple, send me a pen from Heaven." I laughed with my own request but I realized I was late for work so I had to quickly change and go.

Around an hour after being at work, I got a lovely surprise as Ines walked in. Yes, she had returned and I felt genuine happiness at seeing her again, after our hugs and our quick chat about our lives Ines handed me a bag, she had brought me a gift. I was excited, but as I opened the gift, I was astounded.

Inside the wrapping paper was a long white box, and inside the box was a large, pure white feather. It was beautiful; I was speechless when I realized it was a pen!

And so it's time

Out of the many stories I was able to choose from, I have selected only those that I felt would somehow get the chosen message across. I hope I have been able to share with you the simple message that we don't really die, we just swap worlds.

One of my main concerns about writing this book is my fear of raising expectations for my future clients, as I have said, not all readings are sprinkled with magic. Although I now believe that each reading I give is exactly as it supposed to be.

I have been on a lifelong mission to pass on messages to people from their loved ones who are passed and I do my best, even in my failings. I wish I could throw a blanket over this world and cover people in peace and love, I also wish I could lift the veil that stops others from seeing Spirit or the Spirit world as I can, but I realize I am unable to do either of those things. I somehow hope that with this book, it's a small pebble in a pond of ripples that you can open your own heart to peace and love and open your mind to the possibility of Spirit and the Spirit world.

Although I am ever grateful for my gift, I feel that my life purpose was to be a mother. I love loving my children, they may see me as strange or weird on occasion, but hopefully, this book will give them a better understanding of my weirdness.

Till we meet again.

ABOUT THE AUTHOR

Gaynor is currently living in Benidorm in Spain.

She is now working on her next book.

Heaven Is A Real Place

Email

gaynorcarrillo@hotmail.com

If you enjoyed this book, please feel free to leave a review on amazon.

Printed in Great Britain
by Amazon